Church Is Not FOR PERFECT PEOPLE

THE Church IS NOT FOR PERFECT PEOPLE

WILLIAM J. MURRAY

with Al Janssen

HARVEST HOUSE PUBLISHERS
Eugene, Oregon 97402

THE CHURCH IS NOT FOR PERFECT PEOPLE

Copyright © 1987 by Harvest House Publishers
Eugene, Oregon 97402

Library of Congress Catalog Card Number 87-081036
ISBN 0-89081-602-6

Printed in the United States of America.

CONTENTS

FOREWORD

The first year of a completely changed life can be the best or the worst of a man's lifetime. My first year as a Christian was both.

I was 33 years old when I first walked into a church building as a believer. I carried with me a lot of personal baggage in the form of a sinful past. The next three years were spent searching within the church to understand a way of life that was totally foreign to me. What I found many times surprised me. At other times it shocked me. Most of all, those three years taught me to trust God.

The purpose of this book is to discuss what I and other adults discover within the church when we become Christians later in life. The first three years are a period of transition. They are the most crucial years for the new Christian, because he is led in either the right or wrong direction by individuals within the church.

It is my intention to address not only those who are experiencing their infant years within the church, but also those who want to nurture these young Christians. A person like myself who accepts Christ in his late twenties or thirties sees the church from an entirely different perspective than the individual who was raised in the church and accepted Christ at a young age. That's why I call people like me Transition Christians. We see the world and the church differently, and we are also viewed differently by those who have been reared in the church.

It is my prayer that this book will help the new believer in transition and the "old-timer" in the church to better understand each other's thoughts and needs.

—William J. Murray

1

A Startling Contrast

My older daughter hates me. My younger daughter loves me.

My older daughter thinks I'm the worst man who ever walked the face of this earth. My younger daughter thinks I'm a saint.

My older daughter thinks I'm a has-been drunk. My younger daughter has never seen me drink alcohol.

My older daughter never saw me without a cigarette in my mouth. My younger daughter has never seen me smoke.

My older daughter thinks I'm a liar and can't trust me. My younger daughter sees me as someone with whom she can talk, who will give her an honest answer.

My older daughter thinks I took up religion because I was a loser. My younger daughter thinks I'm a winner because I have a relationship with Jesus Christ.

Both daughters are right in their perspectives. Each has legitimate reason for her strong feelings about me.

Perhaps better than anything else, that contrast describes my life since January 24, 1980. On that date my course took a dramatic turn. My older daughter, Robin, hasn't seen me since. She remembers me only as a lying, cheating, boozing, smoking drunk, and she refuses to have anything to do with me. My younger daughter, Jade, was only three years old on that wonderful date. In her home she's known only an honest, loving, caring, sober father. Every time I think of Robin, I am haunted by my past. Every time I look at Jade, I thank God for my blessings and look forward to the future.

Mine wasn't a quiet change that occurred in the privacy of my home. The entire nation heard about it. I was the son of America's most famous atheist—Madalyn Murray O'Hair. I was the reason why prayer was removed from public schools in

9

1963. When I ran into problems with the law, my picture was featured on the front page of every daily newspaper.

What happened to me in 1980 was news. I apologized to the American people for the role my mother and I played in removing prayer and Bible reading from our schools. I apologized for helping to establish the American Atheist Center in Austin, Texas. And I took a public stand by stating unequivocally that I was no longer an atheist. The God of the Bible was now my God. The Man Jesus Christ, who had been only a cuss word in my family, was now my Lord and Savior. The impossible had happened: I had become a Christian.

Jesus said He would divide a man from his father and mother, and that "a man's enemies will be the members of his household" (Matthew 10:36 NIV). That certainly has been true for me. Meeting Christ didn't unite my family; it fractured it. Every time I try to call my mother, she hangs up the phone. Every letter I write to her is either ignored or returned—torn in dozens of little pieces. My wife at the time put up with my "latest thing" for a few months, then split. My younger half-brother thought my conversion was a big joke. My daughter from an earlier marriage had grown up under the influence of my mother; she would have nothing to do with me. All I had left of my human family was Jade, my younger daughter. Only she was willing to love and accept me.

It's true that God replaced my natural family with a new one—the church. But the transition from atheist to church attender hasn't been exactly smooth. The habits and scars of 30-plus years lived totally apart from God aren't overcome in a day. At times the church has struggled to comprehend my past. It is as though I am an alien. We come from totally different worlds. My arrival at the church produced culture shock on both sides.

However, I would never go back to my former life. Just one look at Uncle Irv is enough to remind me of where I would be had I not met Christ. Irv is my mother's older brother. He too has seen the change in my life, but he still doesn't know what to make of it.

It was January 2, 1987, and I was waiting for Irv to step off the plane at Dallas/Fort Worth International Airport. For Christmas I had bought him a plane ticket so he could go to Pittsburgh and spend the holidays with some old friends. After he landed we would have about four hours before we would pick up my daughter Jade, who had spent Christmas with her mother in Florida. Then the three of us would have our belated Christmas celebration.

In 1979 my mother promised to provide Irv with a job and lodging for life at her American Atheist Center. In return, Irv gave her his life savings, mostly money he had received for an accident settlement on his last job.

Two years later, after one of their numerous arguments, my mother had the electricity turned off in Irv's apartment. I was living in Houston then, and Irv called and pleaded for me to come and rescue him. I rented a truck and drove to Austin on a blistering hot August day. When I arrived, the stench from food rotting in his refrigerator was overwhelming, and I had to use a flashlight in order to move his furniture out of the apartment. I helped him reestablish his life in Houston, and later he moved with me to the Dallas area.

For two solid years it was impossible to have a conversation with Irv without him mentioning his sister. She had berated him, cursed him, scolded him, belittled him, and so dominated his life that he could think of nothing except how much he hated Madalyn Murray O'Hair. Now, six years after his escape, those thoughts no longer dominated him, but the emotional scars remained.

Irv could not understand why I gave him 300 dollars each month to supplement his meager Social Security check. While he no longer asked what I expected from him in return, he refused to even consider my explanation that I was only trying to show him the love of Jesus Christ. Every time I mentioned that name, he screamed and stopped his ears with his fingers, as if he were a little child being scolded.

Irv's plane from Pittsburgh was only a few minutes late. From the moment I met him at the gate until we reached the parking lot, I heard more profanity from his mouth than I had heard in the previous 30 days combined. Finally, as I opened the trunk of my car, I said, "Irv, please—I really can't handle that much profanity. You're going to have to tone it down."

Later, as we picked up my daughter and drove out to the house, I told Uncle Irv, "I like to videotape our family opening Christmas presents every year. This will be the first time you've been with us. I don't want profanity on the videotape for my daughter or anyone else to hear. So I would really appreciate it if you didn't swear."

"Don't worry, Bill. I'll just move away from the microphone," he said. That's when the tragedy of his life hit me. My uncle was so used to using profanity that he would rather deprive himself of participation in the ceremony of opening gifts than cease to curse!

At that moment I realized again how, except for the intervention of the Great Physician, I could have wound up just like my uncle. Our backgrounds were virtually identical. Both of us were dominated by our mothers. Both of us had known nothing in our homes but fights, profanity, and shouting. Both of us had endured unending belittlement from our closest family members. Neither of us had any moral foundations. And until 1980, neither of us had experienced anything of the power of God.

Uncle Irv is a perfect picture of a life lived totally apart from God. This man has no concept of decency. He has spent his life drifting, with no sense of purpose. He has tried to find some type of materialistic reality but has no resources with which to ever enjoy material success. He is bound by hatred for his sister and a distrust for all women to the extent that he has refused to enter into any serious romantic relationship. All he can do is swear enough to embarrass a New York City policeman.

I could have been the same. Or worse! While I was growing up, my mother often told me that she didn't care if I became a drug addict or bank robber or if I brought home a boyfriend instead of a girlfriend. *There was only one thing she didn't want me to do in life—become a Christian.* Anything else was fine with her.

It's sobering to realize what I might have done had I not met Jesus Christ. I think of a girl who was raised in much the same type of home as I, one of atheism and Marxism. While my mother was busy removing prayer and Bible reading from schools, this girl's father was founding the Emergency Civil Liberties Union. That's an official legal arm of the Communist Party in the United States. While I had an encounter with God, she became involved in the radical Weather Underground movement which was dedicated to the violent overthrow of the government. Today she is behind bars in a New York prison, convicted of complicity in the triple murder of Brinks armored car drivers and police during a holdup. I know that it's only by God's grace that I'm writing this book instead of standing behind bars like that girl—Katherine Bodin.

I now find it amazing that I actually managed to do fairly well in society even though I lived in a moral vacuum. I carved out a decent career in the airline industry. Sure, I was a ruthless manager, but I did learn a few elements of civility. As I compare Uncle Irv's life with mine, there is really only one significant difference: Jesus Christ has worked in my life as the Great Physician. I've been healed. Irv has experienced no such healing.

That's not to say that the curing process is finished in my life—far from it. Even today, there are many times when I will think of a profane word to say in a frustrating situation. But now, in the overwhelming majority of cases, I do not utter that word. I'm hopeful that someday the Great Physician will cure me completely, so that I will not even think those words. And that's just one area where I struggle to overcome my past and allow Christ to have control.

Maybe you think my life is unusual. It really isn't. Today there are thousands of people like me coming into the church. We did not grow up in Christian homes. We had no moral foundation. Many of us never heard the name of God except in the context of profanity. We never read the Bible. We were abused by our parents, both verbally and physically. We built up deep resentments. When we left home, we lived totally for ourselves, seeking only to please ourselves, without any thought for God. And we discovered that it didn't work. Even if we had material success, we were miserable failures in life.

But now we've met the Great Physician, and He's started the process of transforming us. But we're 25 or 30 or 40 years old, or older. We've picked up an incredible amount of excess baggage. We're materialistic. We've been addicted to substances like alcohol or cocaine or Valium. We've messed up our marriages. We've been governed by our lusts. And our children are heading in the same direction—toward certain destruction—unless there is divine intervention.

I call people like us "Transition Christians." We're adults, and we're new to the church. The one thing we have going for us is that we've finally seen the light. We've found the truth as embodied in the person of Jesus Christ. We've finally come to the cross, experienced forgiveness for our sins, and started over. But we're in a process of transition, because for years we lived life as though God didn't exist.

Is the church ready to accept us? Does it have any understanding of the life we've lived? We've experienced a spiritual birth, but our bodies are damaged by years of abuse and our minds are so thoroughly programmed that our bad habits are very difficult to break. We want to change, but we need help. God may miraculously remove one or more problems from our lives, but we will spend the rest of our lives in the process of change, becoming more like Jesus Christ.

Is the church willing to accept us the way we are right now, still in bondage to some of those old habits? Is the church willing to patiently lead us into the better life, realizing that it will take time—often years—to change? Is the church ready to support us as our families crumble because we are no longer the person our spouse and children once knew? Will the church understand that our kids have known only the world, and will the church encourage us to persevere when our children resist the changes we're trying to make in our homes?

These are important questions, questions with which the church needs to grapple if it truly desires to seek and save the lost. For when the lost meet Christ later in life, they bring a lot of baggage into the church. I know I did. And in the last few years as I've traveled to every corner of the country and overseas, I find that many other Transition Christians also have struggles adjusting to the church. There are a few churches that are havens for such new adult Christians. Many other churches want to reach out and embrace us, but they don't know how. Both sides feel uncomfortable.

Actually, it's a form of culture shock. Transition Christians don't fit easily into the church because we come from a totally different lifestyle. The church has difficulty assimilating us into its fellowship because it doesn't understand how foreign church life is to us. There is a new language to learn, new traditions to observe, new teachings to absorb. Each side needs to understand the forces that are causing tension and adjust. We can do it, but it takes time.

The first step in this understanding is to realize that our backgrounds are different. I mean *totally* different. It took me several years to gain perspective on how radically my life has changed since I met Christ. Sometimes I realize it at the most unexpected moments. Like the time I found myself inside a Las Vegas casino . . .

2

Culture Shock in the Pew

I had been invited to conduct some meetings in Las Vegas during the New Year holidays. The church that was sponsoring the crusade had in its congregation an employee of Circus Circus, a popular hotel-casino. As a result they obtained a very nice room for me at a reasonable price in the towers of the hotel.

As I entered the doors of the hotel, I found myself in the midst of the casino. Then I remembered that in each of the major hotels on the strip, one had to walk through the casino in order to get to the hotel lobby. I had not been in a casino since my conversion, and the last time I had gambled I had won over 4000 dollars at a crap table. That had been nearly seven years earlier.

I was shocked to find myself frozen in the middle of the casino as I took in the sights. My emotions were a whirl of contradictions and questions. Is what these people are doing wrong? I wondered. Is this something that I as a Christian shouldn't do? I noticed the new electronic slot machines. Would it be all right to play five or ten dollars worth of quarters in some of the machines to see how they work? Or is all gambling totally wrong? Is it wrong for these people if it is wrong for me? Is there any in-between category? Is only the *addiction* to gambling wrong, or is it wrong to even dabble in it?

Slowly I forced myself to advance through the room, which was crowded with holiday gamblers. I stopped in front of the crap tables. That had been my favorite game, for the odds were only 51 to 49 against you—the best in the house. I had never felt addicted to gambling, but I did enjoy the excitement. When I had had enough money I had played heavily, trying for a big win. When I didn't have much money, I would play a couple of times just for the free drinks. But where did I stand now that I was a Christian?

Then I looked up and saw several children staring down from the mezzanine area where they could be entertained by

19

the frequent circus shows or lose themselves in the vast array of the latest video games. What impression was this scene making on them? What were they learning? Maybe some of them were watching Dad gamble away their food money for the next month. I thought of my daughter Jade. What impression would this have made on her if I had brought her on the trip? Could I even have stayed here? I shook my head and finally moved into the hotel lobby.

A few minutes later I reached the sanctuary of my room. As soon as the bell hop left I knelt by my bed and prayed, "Lord, what am I to do?" Within a few moments I felt sure that the only right thing for me to do was to not go anywhere near the gaming tables or slot machines, even to watch. I felt better reaching that decision.

That experience was a reminder to me of a fact I have found true in my life, and in the life of nearly every Transition Christian. Every life experience that I went through as a non-Christian I've also had to go through as a Christian. Each time I face such a situation, I have to choose whether I will do it the old way or else respond according to the way Christ would have me live. In the process I see how God has changed me, or sometimes I learn how much work God still has to do in me.

That experience also reminded me of the pull of sin. While I was staying at Circus Circus, I had to drive some distance to the church where I was preaching. On Sunday morning I decided to eat breakfast at the hotel restaurant. However, I had to walk through the casino again to reach the restaurant. And when I arrived at the entrance, there was a long line, even though it was fairly early. With anger I remembered why: The restaurants deliberately kept people backed up into the slot machines so they would play the slots while waiting to be seated. I turned and headed out to my car.

Once off the strip, I stopped at a donut shop and picked up two donuts. They didn't have decaf coffee, so I drove on and stopped at a convenience store to buy my coffee. Inside that store were two slot machines. As I poured my coffee and paid the attendant, I noticed a man in a three-piece suit, with a

Bible under his arm, feeding quarters into the slot machine. Again the questions and emotions swelled within me. Was it wrong for this individual to feed the slots? It seemed to me that if someone had to play a slot machine before church on Sunday morning, then it was quite likely that he had a problem with gambling.

I'm not judging that man. Rather, what I saw is an example of the fact that the world pulls at us, trying constantly to draw us away from our life in Christ. For the lifelong Christian—the person who has grown up in a Christian home, accepted Christ at an early age, and gone to church all his life—that battle is often more discreet. If he has a problem with gambling or alcohol or some other vice, he does it in secret.

But the Transition Christian has openly practiced this lifestyle for years. He's built up strong habit patterns that are difficult to change. And sometimes the church has a hard time understanding that conflict. It expects that the instant a person receives Christ, he is totally transformed. It's true that he is a new person. But the old sin nature remains, and that sin nature doesn't surrender control easily. After all, the old self had total, unrestricted reign for 20, 30, or more years.

That's the conflict the apostle Paul had. I can relate to him when he says, "That which I am doing I do not understand; for I am not practicing what I would like to do, but I am doing the very thing I hate" (Romans 7:15). Paul told of the inner battle he experienced. He didn't do what he knew he should do, and he did what he knew he shouldn't do. He cried out, "Who will set me free?" Of course the answer is that Christ has set us free. It's our job as Christians within the church to help each other experience that freedom. Unfortunately, that process is complicated with what I call culture shock in the pew.

My initial exposure to the church produced all kinds of new questions in areas I had never considered before. For instance, to whom was I married? I got the impression from the Bible that once you were married, God said you could never be divorced in His eyes. Did that mean I was still married to my first wife, Susan? And if so, where did that leave me with

Valerie? Did I have to leave her and try to find Susan? What if Susan had remarried?

If God did recognize my divorce from Susan, there was still the problem of how I had married Valerie. My mother, who was licensed as an atheist minister in Texas, had performed the ceremony. Did God recognize that marriage? If not, did that mean my daughter Jade was illegitimate? It didn't help that Valerie wasn't exactly enthralled by the change in my life. We had married originally because I knew how to show her a good time—like flying first-class to Acapulco for a rousing weekend of nonstop fun. Did my conversion mean we could no longer enjoy a good party?

These questions may seem unusual for a person who has grown up in the church, with lots of Christian friends, and has known only a stable home environment. But for a Transition Christian these are very real and confusing issues. And I didn't know where to find the answers. To make matters worse, I could see that my family probably wouldn't survive. When I had started having problems with alcohol, Val had escaped into a career of her own. She hardly knew me now. Perhaps this was some stage of life I was just passing through. She wasn't sure she wanted to know the new Bill Murray, whoever that was.

Just what had happened to me? I couldn't really grasp it. At times the whole experience was a blur, and I wondered if it had even happened. Every time I heard a preacher give an invitation, I prayed with him and accepted Christ into my life. If I attended church 52 times that first year, then I said 52 salvation prayers at least, and maybe another 52 at home. But that didn't seem to answer my doubts.

I knew there was a God; I knew Jesus Christ was God's Son and had died for me; I knew I had finally stopped drinking alcohol. But was I saved? What did it mean to be saved? Was I really going to heaven? If so, then why did I still have so many bad thoughts? Why was my marriage crumbling? Why was I still addicted to cigarettes? Why did I feel so much guilt about my past? All the sin I had committed so freely over the years was hard to shake. How could I possibly experience the freedom which the Bible promised?

I realize now that my questions are not unusual. The Transition Christian, the person who accepts Christ as an adult, brings a great deal of baggage into his new life with Christ. Sometimes it seems like there are more of us than Christians who know how to help us.

In addition to that inner conflict, life is further complicated for the Transition Christian because of the totally new culture and social life he finds in the church. When I accepted Christ, everything about the church was new: the vocabulary, the social practices, the expectations. No one took me aside and said, "Now, Bill, here's a dictionary of Christian terms. And here's a manual to show you how to act in certain situations." The Transition Christian is on his own unless some sympathetic Christian takes him under the wing and walks him through the process.

Here's just one example. On my first Sunday in the little church I initially attended, I saw this sign in the restroom: "No Smoking Permitted." Why was that sign up? If nobody in the church smoked, why did they need a sign in the restroom? Unless it was meant specifically for people like me. Transition Christians notice things like that, and are confused. Lifelong Christians probably don't even realize the message they're sending.

My smoking habit was a problem for several months after I met Christ. Initially I was smoking three packs of Kools a day. But then I read that menthol cigarettes apparently produced a higher risk of cancer. I wanted to quit and I hated regular cigarettes, so I concluded that maybe if I started smoking something I didn't like, it would be easier to quit. So I switched to Marlboros. I didn't like them, but I still continued smoking three packs a day.

My next step was to switch to something less dangerous—Marlboro Lights. They had one-twelfth the nicotine of Kools. But as I continued to smoke three packs a day, I was going through terrible nicotine withdrawal symptoms. Who was there in the church that I could talk to about my problem? Was there anyone who had gone through this struggle who could help me?

I never found that person, but God took care of it on the morning of July 4, 1980. I awoke at 4:00 that morning and wandered into the kitchen for something to drink. I poured myself a glass of Coke and then reached over and grabbed a pack of cigarettes. I took one out and put it in my mouth, then lit a match. Just as the flame touched the cigarette, I suddenly realized what was happening. I had thought I'd gotten up because I was thirsty, but it was those cigarettes that had awakened me. They had pulled me out of bed in order to force more nicotine into my body.

I stared at that cigarette and realized that I now had a powerful Friend in God, yet I was being controlled by a little object that I could hold in my hand. "No, God, I won't accept this!" I cried. I blew out the match, put the cigarette back in the package, and crushed the pack in my hand. "Lord, You've got to deliver me from this. I cannot be controlled by something I can crush in my own hand." Then I shoved the package into the bottom of the trash can and went back to bed. Since then I've never had a desire for another cigarette. When I got up later that morning, I felt no more effects of nicotine withdrawal. Finally I was free of that habit.

It took six months from the time of my conversion until I was freed from the addiction of nicotine. Other habits took even longer. But how long is the church willing to put up with a habit that most members find offensive? That's the struggle I and so many Transition Christians have to endure. We are born again, but we don't change overnight. We know that some things, like smoking, are definitely not acceptable. But does anyone understand how hard it is to overcome that habit when we've smoked two or three packs a day for 20 years? We want to change, but the body is addicted. We need understanding and help.

It's not just the social habits that are different. Everything about church is so new. For example, the Christianese or Christian slang. Lifelong Christians think nothing of shouting "Amen" at appropriate places during a service. But what in the world does that word mean? It was at least six months before a preacher explained in a sermon that the word "Amen" means "I believe." So when people say "Amen" at the end of a prayer or during a stirring sermon, they are supposedly agreeing with it and believing it for their own lives. I wonder how long some Transition Christians have to go before they learn that fact. For many, it's probably years.

The first time I heard someone call me "brother" in church, I had to resist putting up my fists. You see, the only time I had heard the term "brother" used until then was in a bar. When someone said words like, "Let me tell you something, brother!" that meant you were about to have a fistfight. Naturally, the connotation in the church is much warmer. When someone calls you "brother" or "sister," it is a term of esteem, a way of saying we're equals in the family of God.

I drew a blank the first time I heard someone say to me, "Let's have some fellowship," until I realized he was really saying, "Let's go over to the coffee shop and shoot the breeze." Oh, why didn't you say so!

I have to resist chuckling when I meet a businessman on the plane who says, "Let me share this with you." It's a dead giveaway that the person is a Christian. Christians share ideas rather than saying, "Let me tell you what I think."

These are all rather harmless terms, but Transition Christians have to learn them. People who've grown up in the church have known the language from their youth.

Other adjustments aren't so easy. Even some of the terminology has deeper connotations that I found unpleasant. For instance, I was shocked to discover that there is Christian gossip. It's usually not recognized as such by lifelong Christians, for it's frequently cloaked in prayer requests.

I discovered the ritual in my first adult singles Sunday school class. Part of the time was devoted to sharing of prayer requests. Most of the requests were important—for healing, for financial needs, for work. But a few were questionable. "We really need to pray for John," said one of the girls. "He's fallen away from the Lord the last couple of weeks, and we all see he isn't here today. We need to pray that God will take him out of the things he's involved in."

Red flags went up in my mind. Something was wrong with this request. Maybe it was the insinuations. Has John really fallen away from the Lord? How does she know? If he has, has anyone gone to talk with him and help him? What kind of things is he involved in?

I gradually saw that a few people used prayer-request time in the same way my mother once talked over the back fence with her neighbor. If John had been there, this girl would never have shared that prayer request. It was an insult! It may even have been a cover-up. Perhaps John had taken this girl on a date and then never invited her out again. So she was mad at him but she cloaked her anger in spiritual terms. Even if the request was legitimate, the girl's attitude was wrong. If she was really concerned, she could have said, "I have an unnamed prayer request." She could have gone to the pastor and said, "I think John is struggling and I don't know how to help him. Could you pay him a visit this next week?"

I was also uncomfortable at the assumptions Christians sometimes made. "I'm concerned about John," says someone in the singles group. "I was driving downtown and I saw him go into a gay bar." The implication is that John is doing something wrong. If that's true, then someone needs to help him. But it's also possible that John's job is to service the cigarette machines in the gay bar, or maybe he's a volunteer for Alcoholics Anonymous and he received a phone call to go and pick up a drunk at this bar and drive him home. If we went and talked directly to John, we might learn that the facts are quite different from our assumptions.

"I'm praying for you" is another phrase I found could have negative as well as positive connotations. Once a person said to me, "I'm praying that you'll become interested in dating again." I had never asked this person to pray about my dating life. This person was implying that I wasn't a complete Christian because I wasn't interested in having a relationship with a girl. She didn't ask me what my priorities were. She didn't try to understand my background. She didn't know how much time my ministry took. She simply assumed, based on our limited contact, that God needed to change me in this area.

Now don't get me wrong. Many times when people tell me they're praying for me, it's a real encouragement. And there are people whom I've asked to pray for specific areas of my life and ministry. It means a lot to know they're doing so. But I'm concerned about those people who tell me they're praying about areas of my life that really aren't any of their business. If they really have a burden from God, they might be better keeping that between themselves and God. Or, if they have a legitimate concern that my actions or priorities are wrong, they should come to me in the spirit of Matthew 18:15—"If your brother sins, go and reprove him in private; if he listens to you, you have won your brother."

I had a problem with the whole singles scene in the church. Even before my divorce with Valerie was final, it was clear to me that I was not welcome in the regular adult Sunday school. "This is where you go," they said, pointing to the adult singles group, as though I was being banished to a leper colony. I'm not talking about the younger singles, those in college or early in their career. It's the older singles who are divorced; the Transition Christian gets the message that these people do not fit into the church's social structure. Many adult singles groups seem geared primarily to helping these people find mates, so they can remarry, so they can then join the mainstream of the church.

Another confusing message was when people told me that God had told them things about His will for me. The first time that happened was when a pastor called me and said, "God told me to call you and invite you to speak to our church." Another time a well-meaning woman said, "Bill, God told me that you and Shirley would really look good together." Had God really told them those things? I wanted to obey God, and these people seemed to know Him and love Him. I was confused. Why didn't God tell *me* directly? If God wanted me with Shirley, why didn't I even like Shirley?

By now you may think that I'm antichurch and that all churches are doing it wrong. That is absolutely not the case. I relate all of this to show the often-intense struggles and inner uncertainty that a Transition Christian endures early in his spiritual walk. My intention is not to condemn but to educate. If the church's desire is to reach unchurched people and welcome them into the body, then it needs to understand our background. We don't automatically understand Christian terminology and traditions that lifelong Christians take for granted. Often the message is unwittingly conveyed that we're not welcome, or that we pose an inconvenience. In many cases it wouldn't take much to make us feel welcome.

I'm not unique by any means. Over the years I've talked with many such people who are trying to make sense out of their new life while still battling the old desires of the flesh— like the 32-year-old woman who had lived a life of promiscuous sex and wanted to know why she hadn't lost her lustful desires now that she had accepted Christ. In addition, she was deeply concerned about her 12-year-old daughter, who was just entering puberty. She didn't want her daughter to go down the same path.

Then there was the man who had abandoned his family because of a drug habit. He was saved out of drug addiction and crime, but now his family would have nothing to do with him. Where could he go for support?

Consider the couple that had spent their lives acquiring material wealth and social prestige. They had met Christ, but they still drank. They were confused about what to do with all their material possessions. In addition, their children were vehemently protesting as the parents sought to regain control of the family. "You had your fun, and now you don't want us to have ours," they complained.

There's the woman whose husband had severely abused her physically. She wanted to leave him, but now that she was a Christian she wondered if she had to stay and continue to take the abuse, even when it was potentially life-threatening.

These aren't hypothetical cases. These are people I've talked to recently in churches around the country. They are confused, and they're not sure the church understands. I believe the church *wants* to understand and help, but it doesn't know how. Pastors and Christian workers are sometimes the least equipped to deal with these kinds of problems despite their good intentions. Often they've grown up knowing God's plan. God's ways are such a part of them that they can't comprehend any other kind of life. But Transition Christians have the opposite problem: They grew up without any concept of God, or at best without any practical reality of God's desire to work in their lives.

I was a guest on a Christian television show in Florida. During the show the crew threw a surprise party in honor of the host couple's thirty-fifth wedding anniversary. As part of the surprise, the couple's grown children showed up and praised their parents who had raised them in a godly home. It was a beautiful tribute to people who reflected what a Christian family should be.

During the show I was interviewed by this couple. They asked me to tell how prayer was removed from the schools. During our conversation the woman asked, "But what did your father have to say about all this?"

I glossed over the question by saying, "Well, he wasn't there," and then continued with my story.

A few moments later the lady interrupted me again and said, "But didn't your father do anything to stop this?"

As gently as I could I said, "I need to explain something to you. What happened today on this program was beautiful. It's wonderful that you had a thirty-fifth wedding anniversary, and that you're both involved in ministry on this Christian station, and that your children love you so much that they flew back here to honor you on this occasion.

"Unfortunately, your beautiful family represents a minority of Americans. The overwhelming majority of families aren't like yours. You see, I never had a father. I only met him once. In my home there was violence—with dishes flying through the air—and profanity. In many families the children are beaten or sexually abused, and drugs and alcohol are used. That's the average family in the United States. You are the oddballs. My childhood home represents the average American family. The problems there were average."

I wasn't trying to criticize this woman, but I wanted her to understand that we are ministering to people today who have serious problems. The average evangelistic television outreach doesn't relate to these people. It's too unrealistic. If I had seen that Florida program before I was a Christian, I would have said, "I can't get saved because there's no way I'll ever have a beautiful family like that."

The church as a whole has similar misunderstandings. The impression I got early in my Christian experience was that people in the church don't have the problems I have. I know now that this was a false impression, but nonetheless many Transition Christians struggle because they feel they can never measure up. If there are no alcoholics in the church, how can anyone relate to my struggle with alcohol? If no one struggles with lustful thoughts, then how can anyone help me overcome my lustful past?

Of course, Transition Christians have a false picture of the makeup of the church. The church is made up of sinners saved by God's grace. We're all in the same boat. But the church also tends to have a simplistic view of people's problems. The church needs to realize the tensions and pressures that we face, for we are not completely removed from the world. We continue to face situations like the ones we faced before we met Christ. We desperately want to handle them correctly this time around. But that's hard because we don't come from the same background. People who grew up in the church have a moral foundation, but the Transition Christian frequently comes out of a moral vacuum. Everything about the church is foreign to him.

This is critical to understanding and ministering to the Transition Christian. The church needs to realize that most of us grew up in an amoral or immoral environment. A brief review of my life will serve as an illustration. We'll begin with my mother's attempt to defect to the Soviet Union.

3

DISCOVERING THE MORAL ISSUE

I was barely 14 and my half-brother, Jon, was six when we stood on the deck of the great ocean liner Queen Elizabeth and waved goodbye to my grandparents. As we pulled out of New York harbor, past the Statue of Liberty, and headed into the Atlantic Ocean, I knew we were saying goodbye to a way of life. Mother was escaping what she believed was an oppressive United States government in order to become a citizen of the Soviet Union. The Soviet embassy in Washington D.C. had moved too slowly for her satisfaction, so she had decided that we would sail to France and apply for citizenship in the Soviet Union at the embassy in Paris.

After nearly a month in Paris, we were told that only the Presidium of the Supreme Soviet could rule on our immigration request. That could take months. Then one of the embassy staff members commented on my mother's inability to keep a job for longer than six months. It was illegal to be unemployed in "Rodina" (the motherland). He concluded by saying, "Perhaps you and your children would be better off working for the revolution in your native land."

My mother was almost out of money. She had just enough left to purchase plane tickets back to New York. So in dejection she gave up her attempt and came home.

I told that story when I wrote *My Life Without God* in 1981. At that time I had been a Christian for barely one year and I thought my mother's actions could be explained simply in terms of her Communist, socialist beliefs. Time has provided some additional perspective. I now believe I have a deeper understanding of the pain she endured and how it influenced her actions. I believe that her attempted defection was not due to her political convictions. And neither were the events that followed, for it was shortly after our return that my mother began her battle against prayer and Bible reading in the schools.

Why was my mother so eager to leave the United States? Why was she heartbroken when the Soviet Union wouldn't accept us? Why was she so afraid to live in this country? Those are questions that have intrigued me. And I wondered what impact they had on my life.

We returned to the United States several weeks after school started in 1960. My mother took Jon and enrolled him at Northwood Elementary School in Baltimore. According to standard procedure, the school required a birth certificate for Jon before he could be officially enrolled. My mother said she either didn't have it or couldn't find it. Then she enrolled me at Woodbourne Junior High. We were late arriving, and as we walked down the hall to the school office my mother saw class after class reciting the pledge of allegiance, having a brief reading from the Bible, and reciting the Lord's Prayer. She became livid. Why? Were her convictions so strong that she would take on the whole system because of this issue? At that time I don't believe they were.

Over the next few weeks the administration at Northwood put more and more pressure on my mother to produce a birth certificate for Jon. The more that struggle intensified, the more she attacked my school, demanding that the required period of prayer and Bible reading be abolished. Why was she so insistent? Did she really believe that prayer in school was so evil, or was there a deeper reason? Was there any link between my situation and Jon's at Northwood Elementary? What was motivating this outburst?

Only now, in retrospect, can I see the answer. I could never have observed it as an atheist. And right after my conversion I was still too close to my old life to have the necessary perspective. Only now do I realize that Jon's birth certificate was the reason why prayer and Bible reading were removed from public schools. *Prayer was abolished in public schools not because of my mother's political beliefs, but because of a moral dilemma.*

To explain this, I have to review some family background. Near the end of World War II my mother was involved in a romance with an Army officer named William J. Murray, Jr. It was one of those situations common during wartime, in which both parties were lonely. They became intimate and I was conceived in September of 1945. My father was already married and was part of a wealthy Catholic family. He refused to divorce his wife and marry my mother, and wouldn't even admit to being my father until my mother sued him and the court ordered him to pay child support.

I was born on May 25, 1946, and was named William J. Murray III. Sometime after that my mother began to call herself Madalyn Murray instead of Madalyn Mays, even though my father refused to marry her. I believe this shows just how deeply hurt she was. Sometimes she expressed her pain by telling me she wished I had never been born. I was a constant reminder of the injustice done to her.

In 1954 my mother began dating an Italian man named Michael Fiarello, and she became pregnant again. Once again she was going to have an illegitimate child. Once again the father wouldn't accept responsibility. Perhaps as a statement of her general resentment toward men, my mother determined that she would "teach Mr. Fiarello a lesson." She did it by filling out my brother's birth certificate as follows:

> Name of Father: Michael Fiarello
> Name of Mother: Madalyn Mays
> Name of Child: Jon Garth Murray

She might as well have written the word BASTARD in bright red letters across the face of her son's birth certificate. She could have put any names she wanted to on that piece of paper, since the hospital didn't require a marriage certificate. She could have put her last name and the child's as Fiarello, or the father's name and the child's name as Murray. It was her choice. With all three last names different, my mother was stating for the record what she thought of men and a society that would allow women to be abused by men. At the same time she was condemning herself as a woman of loose morals.

Today in our more permissive culture, society is not so condemning of such a situation. But that wasn't true in the mid-fifties, when my brother was born. My mother was deeply hurt by that stigma. It's understandable that she felt two men had wronged her. They had fathered two children and left her to bear full responsibility for raising them.

That is why my mother attacked prayer in my school. She was *ashamed* of that birth certificate, so she refused to produce it at Northwood Elementary School. She couldn't lash out directly at their rule without drawing attention to her dilemma, so she attacked God instead.

It is my opinion that my mother's maniacal campaign to remove all reference to God in public schools and government, plus her heated atheistic campaigns over the years, stem back to this issue. Madalyn Murray was mad at men, and she was mad at God, who was male. Rather than confront her conscience, she determined to deny God's existence and refused to accept any moral constraints. She had to destroy all reference to God, because if there was a Deity, then He could make demands on her life. From that point on she was at war with God. It was only natural that this had a dramatic influence in my life.

I will admit that most people do not grow up in a home where the mother makes national headlines because of her atheist beliefs. Nevertheless they feel the effects of a godless philosophy just as deeply. If their home refused to acknowledge the existence of God, if Jesus Christ was only a swear word, if arguments were decided on the basis of who could yell the loudest or who wielded the most brute force, if morality was defined only in terms of what one believed was right for himself in that situation, then it's only natural that when the child grew up he would live out those beliefs.

Let me illustrate again from my own life. When I was a boy, my mother consumed most of a gallon bottle of cheap wine each week. It was her way of unwinding. It was also not unusual to see my mother get drunk. At the age of 12 I was invited to have a cup of tea, fortified by a shot of the wine, each night with my mother and grandmother. So from an early age I was taught by example and encouragement that alcohol was fine. When I was 17 and my mother bought me my first six-pack of beer, I consumed it all in one evening. It was no surprise that as an adult I experienced problems controlling alcohol.

I certainly had no moral example or teaching concerning sex. So as soon as I was presented with an opportunity to fulfill my sexual desires, I did. And one day, while I was a senior in high school, my 17-year-old girlfriend, Susan, moved into my room—with my mother's encouragement.

That was the start of a nightmare. On my eighteenth birthday I learned that Susan's father had filed a complaint against me in criminal court for improperly enticing her to leave her home and abandon the Jewish religion. The action would require her not to have any contact with me. My mother's solution was to find a county where we could get married. And then I learned that Susan was pregnant. Some fun it was having no morals! At 18, married and with a child on the way, my plans for the future were dashed.

It's not surprising that at the earliest date possible I would choose to escape from my home and my responsibilities. But that doesn't mean I rejected my upbringing. I didn't know any other life. And even if I had known about God or believed in God, I could not easily have escaped the self-centered moral system I had developed. Like all men and women, I enjoyed sinful self-gratification, and I knew of no reason why I shouldn't indulge to the fullest.

For ten years I had almost nothing to do with my family. My marriage ended in divorce and I ran through a couple of other relationships. Responsibility for raising my daughter was passed to my mother. There were some rowdy periods which are not worth reviewing again in this book. But gradually I began to settle down with a career in the airline industry.

I became a manager for Braniff Airlines and achieved one of the highest productivity levels in the company. I did it because I was a vicious boss. I forced people to give me 100 percent, and when they couldn't give any more I forced them to give another 10 percent. They hated me, yet without realizing it they influenced me.

I made an interesting discovery in the workplace: There were a lot of normal people in the world who worked hard and were generally decent to one another. I began to realize that there was a businesslike way of conducting myself. I didn't have to holler, "Hey, you SOB, up yours!" That was the only way my family dealt with each other. I might have been basically immoral, but I learned how to relate to people without being so abrasive.

Over the years I forgot how horrible my life was as a kid. My youth no longer seemed so bad. In 1975 my mother begged me to move to Austin, Texas, and handle the printing of her magazine and other materials. She really did need help. Her work was in a shambles. Her monthly magazine, *American Atheist*, hadn't been published in years. Her newsletter was mailed very irregularly. Her printing equipment was ruined by the negligence of her husband, Richard O'Hair. Since my daughter Robin lived with her, I thought this was a chance to renew that father-daughter relationship. And now that I was an adult, I figured my relationship with my mother was bound to be better. So I moved.

Over the next two years I helped my mother build the American Atheist Center into a multimillion-dollar operation. Soon after I arrived, the first four-color issue of *American Atheist* rolled off the press. I moved her organization out of a house into a modern office building. I hired several employees to handle materials and process donations.

But my success was accompanied by vicious arguments between my mother and my stepfather, nonstop talking by my brother Jon Garth, and constant criticism, put-downs, and sarcasm from my mother. In that setting life became intolerable. That's when I took seriously to alcohol.

Up until then I drank frequently but not daily. I could work five long hard days, drink Friday through Sunday, and return to work Monday without having to drink again for a few days. But in Austin alcohol became a daily necessity, for I knew of no other way to cope with my situation. By noon I was so exasperated by what was happening in the office that I would slip down to the store, pick up a couple cans of beer, and bring them back to the office to drink. Then I began leaving for the bar at 11:30 in the morning. Over lunch I would down six or seven beers. Then I would pick up a couple of cans to take back to work.

I realize now that there was another problem with my work, for I was not acting like a true atheist. I had an idealistic view of life and I even expressed it in my mother's magazine. I saw myself as a businessman who could bring political power to atheists as a group by doing good things. Why should Christian organizations get all the credit for humanitarian acts? "Don't be surprised," I suggested in *American Atheist* "if, during the next major earthquake, officials of the ravaged country receive a box of canned goods marked: 'Donated by American Atheists. We do not believe in God.' "

It sounded good, but my mother didn't believe it, and neither did most of her friends. For example, I learned that a hospital near Austin desperately needed a certain piece of medical equipment. Mother's organization now had plenty of cash, so I suggested that we donate 70,000 dollars for the purchase of that new machine. We would call a big press conference and show the world that atheists could be charitable too. It would do wonders for our image.

But Madalyn Murray O'Hair wouldn't hear of it. No, that money had to go to far more "important" uses, such as lawsuits to remove "In God We Trust" from our money and to prevent prayer by our astronauts in space. The goal of atheism was to destroy religion. Money couldn't be wasted on frivolous things like hospital equipment that might help save people's lives.

I didn't want to believe that all atheists thought that way. So I wrote to about 400 members of my mother's organization with whom I had had personal correspondence. I asked for their support of positive rather than negative atheism. I suggested that we use funds to establish atheist chairs at universities rather than to sue to have religious chairs removed. I recommended construction of monuments and hospital wings. A handful of people sent contributions out of habit. But the overwhelming majority of those who answered my letter pelted me with such abuse that I was stunned. Over and over they reminded me that the principal goal of atheism was the destruction of religion.

Finally I couldn't stand it anymore. I had to escape from that negative environment. I took my wife and new daughter, Jade, to Houston, where I went back to work in the airline industry. But one very good thing did come out of those two years in Austin. Somehow in the midst of that hell—I can't tell you exactly when or how—I started believing in God. In fact, I even talked to Him. Whether it could be considered prayer or not, I don't know. But I realized that if there were people in this world as wicked as I and my mother were, then there had to be God, a force for good that could counteract evil. And to that God I cried, "Get me out of this mess!"

Soon after I moved to Houston I attended my first Alcoholics Anonymous meeting. If I had truly been an atheist at that point I would have walked out, for among the first things AA required was that I admit I was powerless over alcohol, that I believe that a Power greater than myself could restore me to sanity, and that I make a decision to turn my will and my life over to the care of God as I understood Him. That's not exactly a call to faith in Jesus Christ, but it was more than I had ever considered doing up to that time. Because I was raised so totally opposed to any concept of deity, my reaction should have been, "If I've got to accept God in order to get sober, forget it!" I should have left and bought myself a bottle. But I stayed. And I listened.

With the help of AA I stayed away from alcohol for four months before starting again. It was a constant battle. I would go three or four weeks without a drink, but then a crisis or an argument with my wife would cause me to drink again. I had good intentions; I wanted to change and please God. But I seemed powerless to maintain any consistency.

In August of 1979 I became manager of the hub station of a large commuter airline out of San Francisco. Then in December I was hired by a major airline to be their station manager. My wife and daughter stayed in Houston while I lived in San Francisco and flew home to the family once or twice a month. Now my search for God became more intense. I even attended several churches. But there seemed to be a barrier that prevented me from reaching Him.

Ironically, AA, which turned me away from alcohol, was probably that barrier between God and me. I was told to turn my life over to God "as I understand Him." I certainly didn't have much understanding. I didn't know a *living* God. Yet I sensed that there was a God who was alive and real. AA didn't have the complete answer for me, but I was comfortable at AA and perhaps that prevented me from searching harder.

Then on the night of January 24, 1980, I had an incredible dream. In the midst of that dream a great winged angel stood in front of me with a sword in his hand. Inscribed on the sword's hilt were the words "IN HOC SIGNO VINCE," meaning "By this symbol conquer." The tip of the sword's blade pointed down and touched an open Bible.

I awoke and realized that my quest for God would end within the pages of the Holy Bible, the very Book my mother had helped ban from devotional use in the public schools of the United States. I climbed out of bed, dressed, and drove into San Francisco to an all-night discount department store near Fisherman's Wharf. There, under a stack of porno magazines, I found a Bible. I bought it, took it back to my apartment, and began to read the Gospel of Luke. There I found my answer—not the Book itself, but Jesus Christ. He had done something for me by dying on the cross.

It was obvious that I was losing control of my family situation. I desperately wanted to get control over my drinking; I had just had my last drink less than 48 hours earlier. I knew that a drastic change was necessary in my life. I didn't know how that change would occur, but I now knew that Jesus held the answer. With that I cried out, "Jesus, I want to be with You instead of what I'm doing!" I know now that this wasn't much of a salvation prayer, but it was heartfelt. And it was a start.

What does a man do after such a dramatic conversion? Initially I had welcomed the job in San Francisco as a chance to escape from my marital problems. Now I wanted to go home and try to repair my family. In addition, I was forced to work on Sundays, so I was not able to go to church on any regular basis. I knew no Christians. I was struggling to understand what had actually happened to me spiritually. And I was also battling my health, which had deteriorated because of the years of heavy drinking, long work hours, and the fact that I continued to smoke three packs of cigarettes daily.

There was an additional struggle: No one knew I was a Christian. How long could I keep this a secret? Should I keep it secret? What would happen if the media found out that the son of America's best-known atheist had become a Christian? And if they did find out, would that publicity cost me my job? Right now everyone still thought I was an atheist. How could I continue to let them think that? I began to realize that I had to take some kind of stand.

There was another reason why I needed to go public. I was feeling the pull of the world again. What would keep me from taking another drink? If I had one beer or a glass of wine, I knew what would happen; I would sink again into that downward spiral. But if I took a public stand, maybe that would be a strong deterrent to keep me from slipping back into my former lifestyle.

It all came to a head on February 10 when I wrote letters to *The Baltimore Sun* and *The American Statesman* in Austin, Texas. To the people of Baltimore, I apologized for the part I played in the removal of Bible reading and prayer from the public schools. To the people of Austin, I apologized for the role I played in establishing the American Atheist Center in their city:

> I would like to apologize to the people of Austin
> for the part I played in the building of the personal

empire of Madalyn O'Hair. My efforts to that end were an affront to the people of Austin, the people of this nation, and to God.

My crime was twofold in that I was aware of the wrong of my actions at the time and continued them for the purpose of my financial profit. I was continuing to practice the hateful and antimoral way of life I had learned from birth in an atheist home. . . .

Looking back on the 33 years of life I wasted without faith and without God, I pray that I may be able to correct just some of the wrong I have created. The part I played as a teenager in removing prayer from public schools was criminal. I removed from our future generations that short time each day which should rightly be reserved for God. Inasmuch as the suit to destroy the tradition of prayer in school was brought in my name, I feel gravely responsible for the resulting destruction of the moral fiber of our youth that it has caused.

When those letters were finished, I sealed them in envelopes, stamped them, and placed them by the door so I could mail them in the morning. It was 11:00 and I went to bed. But I couldn't sleep. An unexpected turmoil began seething within me. On the one hand I sensed God telling me to mail those letters. On the other hand I worried about the public response. The newspapers could make a big deal of this. I had a good job and I didn't want to lose it because of adverse publicity.

The more I tossed and turned, the more I realized that if those letters weren't mailed immediately, they weren't going to be mailed—ever. This was a critical moment. Either I stepped out and stated once and for all that I was now a Christian or else I turned away and went on as though nothing had happened.

But something *had* happened. I couldn't deny it.

At 2:00 A.M. I got up, got dressed, grabbed the letters, and got in my car. I drove from my apartment in Burlingame all the way to the Air Mail Facility at San Francisco International Airport. When I dropped the letters off there, I knew there was no possibility of retrieving them later. Before dawn they would be on an airplane. As soon as I sent them on their way, I felt a tremendous burden lifted off me.

The next day at work I got a call from company headquarters in Nashville ordering me to close the San Francisco station. I had one week to lay off all the employees and ship the equipment and supplies back to Nashville. I followed the orders, returned the rental furniture in my apartment, and flew home to Houston. Of course, when I had written those letters, I had put the Burlingame address down as the return address. When the Baltimore and Austin papers received the letters, it took them nearly two months to track me down in Houston.

God knew what He was doing by moving me and delaying the publication of those letters. That allowed me to attend church and start getting my feet on the ground spiritually before I was launched again into the public eye. Almost immediately after those letters were published in May, I was asked to go to Washington D.C. to appear with Jerry Falwell and Senator Jesse Helms in support of a constitutional amendment for school prayer. Then invitations to speak followed, and it became difficult to receive the kind of teaching I needed as a very young Christian.

Christians who have known the Lord for many years have difficulty comprehending the pressures on a new adult Christian. One thing all Christians need to remember is that *we are saved out of sin*. Before we were Christians, the Bible says we were slaves to sin. Now, as Christians, we no longer have to give in to sin. That's what the gospel is all about. That's the message that hit me like a sledgehammer—*Christ died on the cross for sinners!* We don't deserve heaven, and the only way to heaven is through the sacrifice that Christ made for us. I didn't need to be convinced of my need for Christ; Transition Christians know they are sinners. It's very clear what Christ is offering them—freedom from their sinful past.

There was a woman who called me while I was on a talk show. On the radio she said, "With all the sin you were involved in, I just don't understand how you could have accepted Christ."

"That's why!" I practically shouted. "The question is how do you find Christ if you've never been exposed to sin? Christ didn't die on the cross for sinless people."

That's what confuses Transition Christians at times—we wonder how some Christians reared in the church ever got saved. In some churches we literally get the impression that no one in this congregation ever did anything wrong. Of course, that's not true—everyone has sinned. But that's not the message we get. We wonder how a person could be saved if the worst thing he ever did was jaywalk.

It was only over time that I realized that growing up in the church doesn't mean that people aren't sinners. Many times they've simply learned to disguise their sin. The average worldly, materialistic sinner doesn't hide his sin. Heathen alcoholics go openly to the bars and drink, but a Christian who develops a drinking problem has to hide it. You rarely see him going in and out of the local bars. At church he appears happy and sober.

The average worldly sinner doesn't try to hide his sexual activity. But the fundamentalist Christian won't admit he has ever lusted after a woman—except Jimmy Carter, who admitted it in *Playboy*. If these Christians are such good, wonderful people, why did Christ die for them? It took me a long time to figure out that *all* of us are sinners. It's just that for some of us it's more obvious.

Recently I was in St. Louis and on the front page of the *Post-Dispatch* was an article about Arthur L. Mallory, State Commissioner of Education, admitting he had a drinking problem after he was arrested for shoplifting wine from a supermarket shelf and drinking it in the rest room. Why did this respected state official do this? Because he was ashamed: "I am a Southern Baptist deacon and Southern Baptist deacons don't buy wine."

I wonder how many Christians feel like him. "I guess I've never admitted that I had a drinking problem," Mallory was quoted in the article. "I can't tell you how difficult it is for me to admit that I'm wrong. I'm sorry. I've felt that I should not have faults." But, of course, we all have faults. Transition Christians are very aware of the fact they are sinners. But sometimes lifelong Christians either can't admit their faults, or feel they must hide them.

I believe there are a large number of unsaved people in fundamental, evangelical churches. Oh, maybe they walked forward at age seven or eight and got baptized. But by the age of 15 they didn't understand what they did or why they did it. Often they went forward just because some of their friends did; it was the thing to do.

I've probably offended some readers with that last paragraph. How can I possibly say that? I say it because I am continually astounded at how many deacons come forward when I give an evangelistic invitation. In fact, once the wife of a pastor came forward. In a typical church where I give an invitation, one-quarter to one-half of those who come forward and accept Christ have been in that church for many years, and everyone *assumed* they were saved.

One deacon confessed, "For 25 years I haven't known whether or not I was saved. I went forward when I was eight because everyone else did. But I never invited Christ into my life. In fact, I steal money from the offering every Sunday." *That man was finally admitting his sin*. Now he was ready to be saved because he understood his need for Christ.

Satan would really like us to miss this point. I can speak from experience. For nearly a year I wasn't sure if I was a born-again Christian. I had already written my letters to the newspapers. I was speaking in churches. I was being invited on Christian talk shows. But I didn't know for sure if Christ had come into my life. Satan was trying to take away the joy of that great moment in San Francisco. And he almost succeeded.

During that year I must have said 100 salvation prayers, asking Jesus to forgive my sins and come into my life. I knew I couldn't continue living with such uncertainty. Finally I told myself, "God is in the business of saving sinners. Did not the lowly publican in Luke 18 find grace while the 'good' Pharisee's prayer wasn't even heard?" I had confessed the gospel publicly as God told me to do in Romans 10:9—"If you confess with your mouth Jesus as Lord, and believe in your heart that God raised Him from the dead, you shall be saved." So I was as saved as the publican in Christ's parable.

With that issue settled, I could finally move on with my Christian walk. My confusion when I was a new Christian motivates me to try to prevent similar confusion with people who attend my crusades. In my initial invitation I have people follow me in a salvation prayer while they remain seated. Then I invite those who prayed with me to stand and come forward. "There's someone out in the parking lot who wants a ride home with you tonight," I explain. "That person is Satan. He's standing beside your car right now, waiting to get his hands on you. He wants to tell you that your experience tonight isn't real. He wants to convince you that you're not saved. The best way to make sure Satan doesn't ride home with you tonight is to make a public statement that you are now living for Christ."

The battle that I and other Transition Christians have questioning our salvation experience is not a new one. You can still see a large ink stain on the wall of Martin Luther's home in Germany. That's where he hurled an inkwell in order to strike Satan, who was telling him that he was doing the wrong thing. If Satan can be that real to Martin Luther, then he certainly can be that real to people today. That's why I advise that if you've said a salvation prayer and asked Christ to come into your life and forgive your sins, and you've publicly stated that you now intend to live for Christ, then assume you're saved and act accordingly.

Even after they gain assurance that Christ has come into their lives and forgiven their sins, Transition Christians face an ongoing struggle with their past. Janet (not her real name) was a recent divorcee who had destroyed her marriage through a promiscuous lifestyle. With her two-year-old child, she attended one of my crusades and met Christ. She started attending church and got involved in the singles ministry.

One day Janet called me. The previous Sunday the pastor had preached a powerful sermon on the subject of being separated from the world and living for Christ. She was deeply moved, for that was her intense desire. As soon as the sermon was finished, the assistant pastor made some announcements. One of them was a reminder for the singles to sign up for the ski trip scheduled for the following weekend. Sounds innocent, right? How could this possibly cause any problems in the congregation?

"Bill, I don't think I should go on this ski trip," Janet told me. "The last time I went skiing with a group of couples, I allowed two men to . . ." Her voice trailed off, but I got the messsage. "What's going to happen to me if I go?" she pleaded. "How can I be sure I'll remain pure? I want to maintain my spirituality."

"Have you talked with your pastor?" I asked.

I already knew what her answer would be. "No. I don't know how I could tell him my struggle." I knew she was right. To the lifelong Christian there was no conflict. The ski trip was an innocent way to get singles together for a good time. It probably never entered his mind that there might be a problem. How could she go to him and say, "Pastor, I'm afraid to go on that trip because I might want to have sex with a man"? So who does she go to? Her 50-year-old singles Sunday school class teacher who's trying to get her married off? Does she go to the assistant pastor, who's a third-generation minister?

"Janet, let me suggest something that I hope is helpful," I said. "Since I've been saved, I've had to go through nearly every life experience that I went through before I was saved. Before I was saved I had a child who got sick; after I was saved I had a child who got sick. Before I was saved I was tempted by alcohol; after I was saved I was tempted by alcohol. Before I was saved I was tempted by sex; after I was saved I was tempted by sex.

"Each of those situations needs to be met individually. It is important to go through each situation in life again as a Christian, and *not cave in*. In this way, as we see God give us new responses, we start building new habits."

Encouraged that God could help her, she went and had a fun and wholesome trip. Now I can imagine someone reading this book thinking, "But what if she hadn't resisted the temptation?" Some might think I gave her poor advice. I agree that there are times when we need to flee a situation where we know we are too weak to resist. But I also knew this woman's heart, and I felt she needed to experience the Christian victory she could have in that group setting. The point of this illustration is that Janet needed encouragement, but no one in her church even realized she had a struggle. What if a mature single Christian woman had said to Janet, "Let's go on this ski trip together; I'll room with you and we'll be together the whole time, and we'll have a lot of fun"? That's what she needed.

There's another very crucial issue for the Transition Christian—his children. The Transition Christian knows what life is like without Christ. And he doesn't want his children to suffer from the same mistakes that he made. But that's not so easy. If one parent is Christian and the other isn't, there's going to be tension in this area. If one or more children are teenagers, they may already have started down the wrong road. What can a parent do to maximize the possibility that his children will choose the right path?

4

PROTECTING THE CHILDREN

Whenever possible, I like to take my music department with me when I'm invited to speak. It's a lot of fun to get up in a church and say, "All evangelists have a music department in their ministries these days. Tonight I'm happy to announce that I have my entire music department with me. So before I speak, I'd like to invite my music team to come up right now and perform." With that, my daughter Jade bounces up to the stage, takes the mike, and wows the crowd with a couple of wonderful Christian songs.

By the time she was nine years old, my daughter had performed in front of crowds in excess of 3000 people. One pastor even inquired about her coming back to his church and doing an entire concert—without her dad preaching. I'm not quite sure how I feel about that! But I can say that one of my greatest joys in life is having a wonderful relationship with my daughter. After all I've been through, I finally have a family relationship that is not full of acrimony.

As I look at my beautiful daughter and admire her talents as a singer, ice skater, computer whiz, and "A" student, I am so thankful that she has never been exposed to the lifestyle that was such a part of my youth. Unfortunately, my older daughter, Robin, has never known anything else. Early in her life she learned that things like homosexuality, lesbianism, alcohol, drugs, euthanasia, and abortion are acceptable because it's all a matter of personal preference. Many of those things are glamorized on television. My mother's atheist conventions actively promote them. Schools teach that there are no moral absolutes and that each person must decide what morals he will incorporate in his own life.

It's my fault that Robin was raised in an atheist home. When I was a young man I didn't want to accept the responsibility for her. It was more fun to have my freedom, so I turned her over to my mother and lost her as a result. I'm not about to let that happen again. Jade's exposure to that kind of atheistic, humanistic philosophy has been minimal. For as long as she can remember, she's attended church. She's accepted Jesus Christ as her Lord and Savior. She loves God and cannot comprehend supporting the concepts that her grandmother and older sister so staunchly uphold.

My greatest concern in life is that Jade never have to go through the hell I endured. My heart aches knowing that Robin must face daily confrontations with absolutely no moral ground to stand on. I don't want Jade to have to go through that. Fortunately, I still have the opportunity to direct her life so that hopefully this won't happen.

I believe my concern is typical of Transition Christians who have children. If a person's house is on fire, he will try to save everyone in it and his most important possessions. But who or what will he rescue first? Usually he tries to save his children above all else. That is also true spiritually.

When I met Christ, naturally I wanted everyone in my family to experience the joy of that relationship. I certainly didn't want my marriage to fail. It was my desire to see Valerie, Jade, and me become a united Christian home. But that didn't happen. I can't condemn Valerie for that. I caused her a lot of physical and emotional pain over the years. When I met Christ, she was immersed in her own career and we scarcely saw each other. Besides, Christ made me a different person and she had difficulty relating to the new Bill Murray. Val had married an airline executive who could show her a great time. My salary furnished us with all the nice materialistic accommodations of life. As a Christian, my priorities changed. The church rather than materialistic gain and parties became the center of my life. I also had a desire to be in the ministry. Those were not things that interested Valerie.

Frankly, that's true of most Transition Christians because when one adult in the home accepts Christ, there usually is a moral split. Suppose a couple were both heavy users of alcohol, or were involved in wife-swapping. Then one partner is saved, but the other wants to continue in the same activities. *I can guarantee that there will be conflict.*

Suppose a couple is totally materialistically inclined. Suddenly the wife is saved and insists on giving 10 percent of the gross of their business to the church. You can imagine what the husband is going to think! Add to this the fact that neither parent has given much supervision to the children. The children have been taught, "You can do whatever you want as long as you don't go overboard. We don't care if you drink a little alcohol; just don't get drunk. We don't care if you use a little marijuana, but stay away from the hard drugs. Sex is okay in moderation; just make sure you use some form of birth control." That's the typical humanist approach to life.

Now one parent has a different value system. And that parent wants to change the rules for the children, because now *it matters*. Which parent do you think the child wants to listen to? The one who says a little bit of anything is okay, or the one who says that God has a standard and a little bit of marijuana or a little bit of sex before marriage is not okay? The older children will most certainly protest. And the non-Christian parent will probably support them. Given a clear choice, man is going to move toward sin. That's human nature when it's not under God's direction.

These conflicts should not surprise us. Jesus said, "Do you suppose that I came to grant peace on earth? I tell you, no, but rather division; for from now on five members in one household will be divided, three against two, and two against three" (Luke 12:51,52).

The implications of this issue are great. For example, take the child who has a parent who's an alcoholic. Twenty to 25 percent of all men and 5 percent of all women who have alcoholic relatives will become alcoholics themselves. In addition, it's a fact that most people who accept Christ do so in their youth.

I'm glad that God isn't governed by statistics. If he can bring me to Himself at age 33, then anyone can come at any age. But reality suggests that if I have to choose between winning my spouse to Christ and winning my child, my chances are significantly better if I focus on my child.

There's a family in the Northeast that illustrates the impact of this issue across three generations. Every time I'm in their community to speak, Mrs. A pleads with me to come and talk to her husband. Inevitably, as I arrive at their home Mr. A leaves via the back door.

Mr. A is basically a good man. He runs a small business that is successful to the point where he is semiretired. He spends most of his evenings playing cards with some friends—for small stakes that rarely exceed 10 or 15 bucks. He believes that if he accepts Christ he will have to give up all his friends and his way of life. In reality, he's really not doing that much wrong. In fact, he might be surprised to learn that a couple of his card-playing friends are actually Christians.

This couple has two grown children. The younger son could best be described as an Irish stud, a good-looking man with a Playboy symbol hanging from his car mirror who wants only to enjoy the good life. Amy, his older sister, attends church three times a week, is divorced, and has one daughter. Amy's overriding concern is for her child, that she not make the same mistake Amy made by an ill-advised marriage to a non-Christian.

How did Amy wind up with a poor marriage? Because *her mother didn't make sure she was taught how to develop good relationships with Christian men.* You see, Mrs. A met Christ and started attending church when her daughter was a young teenager. Since she had never required her children to go to church before, she decided there was no reason to start now. That was a serious mistake. Now there is another broken home because the daughter had no Christian training in the home.

The length of the marriage and the age of the kids will have an effect on the stability of the home when one partner meets Christ. If the marriage is fairly young, my observation is that unless both partners accept Christ, the marriage rarely survives. If there are children between the ages of five and 15, there's a higher chance of the marriage lasting for the sake of the kids, even when one parent doesn't believe in Christ. If the children have left home or are about to leave home, once again the marriage will have a higher chance of failure when one partner meets Christ, for the children will no longer be a factor in holding the home together.

So what is a parent who's a new Christian to do? Should he or she change the ground rules and require the child to go to church and Sunday school? Should he change the rules in the home? Should he pull a child out of public school and enroll him in a Christian school? My answers are: Yes, maybe, and it depends. Let's look at the issue of how we can best help our children avoid our mistakes, and hopefully meet our God in the process.

First, let's recognize the kinds of people coming into the church in this situation. Many of them are of the baby-boom generation, and often they're having children late in life. A lot of women aren't having their first child until they're 30 years old. Then they get into their late thirties and realize that sin isn't fun anymore. That's the problem with sin: It always feels good at the start, but once it no longer feels good, you're trapped. I see a lot of women like this coming into the church in their mid-thirties with children between the ages of five and ten. Often they're single. They're the easiest to minister to because they know their mistakes. They see the problems caused by their lifestyle, and usually the child is young enough to be turned around.

Bobbie Jean is a good illustration. She was a typical "new breed" Texas girl who was reared in a public school system which taught her to look out for herself first. By the age of 27 she was a sales manager for Southwestern Bell Telephone. She was successful but alone. So she decided to have a baby, but didn't want to get married because she didn't want a man "in her way."

With an eye for the future appearance of her child, Bobbie Jean selected and seduced a handsome young man. She had a son, but six years of raising a child alone taught her that she had made a mistake. A friend at work talked her into placing her little boy in a Christian school where he would not be exposed to the same false moral education they both had been taught. Once exposed to the church through the school, Bobbie Jean accepted Christ and quickly put her life and her son's life in order.

More difficult is the single head of family who shows up with two or three kids that span several years—especially when one is a teenager. The teenager usually has intellectualized the situation: Mommy was a drunkard; Mommy was promiscuous; now Mommy doesn't want me to have any of the fun because she's getting old and ugly. That teenager is headed in the direction of the world. However, the youngest child is often still loyal, and the one in the middle isn't sure which way to turn. This family needs a good deal of counseling.

Often the oldest child will rebel and refuse to go to church. He doesn't want to give up the world. And it's even harder if he's living part of the time with the other parent who is reinforcing the old way of life.

In this case the Christian parent must do everything in her power to get the teenager involved in the church. Being a new believer, the parent cannot provide the training the teenager needs. This teenager needs to belong to a group which can provide positive peer pressure. That positive pressure can only be found in the church, not in the world.

What if both parents are together and they have younger children? If both accept the Lord, then that's ideal. The younger children will usually adjust to the church. But if they have older children, particularly teenagers, then there are problems. The kids are saying, "Mom and Dad are getting old and they can't get involved in all the things they used to be involved in, so now they want to ruin my fun." Of course the children don't understand all the pain that went with the "fun" their parents had, and probably wouldn't accept any explanation.

One couple told me that their 16-year-old boy refused to go to church with them. "All he does is spend his money on albums by the Twisted Sister and WASP (We Are Sexual Perverts). He sits up in his room playing those records. We think he may be using drugs. Now that we're Christians, we've bought him some Christian rock albums, but he won't listen to them. He absolutely refuses to participate in family activities. We're concerned about the example he's having on his younger brother."

As they poured out their tale of woe, I finally asked them, "Pardon me, but I think I'm missing something here. Is this your teenage son's home, and you're simply living with him?"

"Why, no, of course not," they answered. "It's our home."

"Oh, then he pays rent for his room?"

"No, we provide everything for him."

"Then I don't understand your problem. You've told me this is your home, yet you have no control over the people who live in it. Aren't you supposed to set the rules for your home? If you find your son's music offensive, then pack it up and take it out. If he's not conducting himself the way you want him to, then tell him exactly what you expect him to do and make him do it."

"But he might leave if we do that. What if he leaves?"

"Your family would probably be better off. Remember, you've got a younger child who is watching this. If he has a choice of following the road to godliness or the road to sin, which one do you think he'll take? It's your responsibility to either change your son or let him move out. Besides, your son is more likely to respect you if you take a stand."

"But I don't know if I could take it if he leaves."

"He'll probably come back. You see, he's going to find that his lifestyle doesn't work so well without the support of a godly home. It's a tough way to learn a lesson, but he'll learn it. One way or another, you've got to bring it to a head."

This couple accepted my advice. After a several-month struggle of wills, the teenager developed a respect for his parents and confessed a drug problem, which has now been successfully treated. He no longer listens to his heavy-metal albums. The parents had to love this young man enough to be tough on him. And it worked!

The next case is where both parents are together, but only one has accepted Christ. We looked at one case earlier, with

Mr. and Mrs. A. We've seen the result where the mother didn't do anything. The son is a playboy, the daughter has a ruined marriage, and a granddaughter hangs in the balance.

Most churches are not equipped to minister to this family. Mrs. A and Amy each need counseling or some kind of support group, and the pastor needs to pay a visit to Mr. A. Let me say that when this doesn't happen, especially if there are teenage girls in the home, the child's morals are confused, and she brings those confused morals into the church. It's devastating to the teen environment of that church. Unfortunately, I've met a lot of loose women in the church who know the Bible inside and out. They know what's right and wrong, but the ungodly influences are so great that they can't seem to resist temptation. According to Josh McDowell, *60 percent of Christian young people are sexually active today!*

A similar situation is where the parents are separated or divorced, but they have joint custody. When one parent is a Christian and the other isn't, the child is divided between two value systems. In both cases the parents need to set aside their differences and talk things out for the sake of the children. The kids need to have one standard that's enforced by both Mom and Dad. The Christian spouse needs to initiate the discussion, saying something like this: "I know you're not a Christian, and I can't make you become one. But let's think about what's best for our kids. Surely they don't have to make the same mistakes we made." The non-Christian partner may agree that the child needs to go to church and may support that decision.

Sometimes this cooperation does not exist, so the two value systems compete for the mind and soul of the child. Because the Christian parent is dealing with the eternal destiny of the child, that parent must do everything in his power to expose the child to a godly lifestyle and education.

With Jade, I made sure she participated in church activities. That was easy; she enjoyed going to church. When she was six I sent her to Word of Life Camp, and there she made her decision to live for Jesus Christ. She made it willingly, without any pressure from me. Sure, I wanted her to do that, but I realized that only *she* could make that decision. My responsibility was to put her in the environment; God did the rest.

The area of education should be a major concern to the Christian parent. Perhaps more than most people, I am acutely aware of the philosophy that pervades our system of public education. After all, my family is part of the reason for the problem. Don't believe for a moment that there isn't religion taught in the public schools. There is religion, and that religion is secular humanism.

Most of America does not know what secular humanism is. That is why it is the most dangerous religion in the world today. It has a tremendous effect on our public education, for our textbooks and curriculum are based primarily on humanism. For example, it means that evolution instead of creationism is taught, for humanism holds that the universe is self-existing, and that man is simply a part of nature that has emerged as a result of a continuous evolutionary process.

In 1983 the National Commission on Excellence in Education issued its report, which included this shocking statement: "If an unfriendly foreign power had attempted to impose on America the mediocre educational performance that exists today, we might well have viewed it as an act of war. As it stands, we have allowed this to happen to ourselves."

Samuel L. Blumenfeld has detailed in his book *N.E.A.: Trojan Horse in American Education* how that mediocrity emerged and developed. He shows how our system of public education has come under the control of people whose values are totally opposed to Christianity. Blumenfeld writes:

> Public education is firmly and irrevocably controlled by the behavioral scientists, who control the graduate schools, teacher training, curriculum development, textbook writing, professional publications and organizations, federal programs, and the largest private foundations. The thousands of doctoral students who pour out of the psych labs and

graduate schools of education are now the profes-
sors and social scientists who run the system. It is
impossible to truly reform public education without
separating it from behavioral science.[1]

Behavioral science and the religion of humanism has a
tremendous effect on the teaching of moral values. The
Humanist Manifesto II states, "Ethics is autonomous and
situational, needing no theological or ideological sanctions."
Therefore public school teachers are instructed not to take any
position on right and wrong. Rather, they are to help students
"clarify" their own values. It's all a matter of personal preference. This philosophy teaches that the individual is the final
source of judgment on almost all issues, and that values are
determined "out of personal choices." Ultimately, values clarification teaches that self-fulfillment is the ultimate goal of the
individual. It's a religion that teaches that each man, not God,
is the center of his universe. There are no absolutes. Right and
wrong do not exist.

My daughter Jade was in first grade when she was first
exposed to values clarification. One evening I was talking to
her about a situation where she needed to change her behavior. She promptly informed me, "That's what you believe.
Don't force it on me." That wasn't my daughter speaking, but
the school system. She was simply parroting what she had
heard. I knew then that I had to get her out of that school
and into a setting that would at least be supportive of my
position as a Christian parent. Having a Christian home
wasn't enough; I needed to provide a school environment that
cultivated her spiritual and moral development.

Deciding where my daughter should go to school was more
difficult. I knew that not all public schools are bad. There are
many rural schools where the discipline and academics are just
as good as in a good private school. But generally that is not
true when you get around the large cities. Since I wasn't in a
position to teach her at home, this meant that my options were
to send her to a Christian school or to a private school that
upheld the values I considered important.

I did some research and found two high-quality Christian schools in the city that would challenge my daughter's bright mind and give her the quality of athletic and extracurricular activities that she desired. Unfortunately, each required us to travel across town more than one hour in each direction. I didn't think it was fair to submit Jade to two hours of commuting every day.

There were quite a few smaller Christian schools, most of them tied to churches, that used a curriculum where the child could progress at her own pace. Typically such a school had very limited resources. The teachers often weren't qualified to teach in certified schools. There was a lack of athletic facilities or programs. The library had only a hundred books. Science equipment was nonexistent. Computers were unheard of or were considered a tool of Satan. I could imagine Jade graduating from high school with an eighth-grade education, knowing the Bible and little else.

Maybe that sounds harsh, but I couldn't even consider putting my daughter in an inferior academic environment. As I explored other options, I found a private school that was highly acclaimed for its academics, provided the proper discipline, had high-quality athletic and extracurricular programs, and even offered a program for after-school hours for those kids whose parents worked late. It was the ideal situation. In order to get a comparable Christian school, we would have had to commute four hours every day. I decided that as far as Jade's spiritual education was concerned, I and the church could provide that.

My point in reviewing all this is that the Transition Christian has a responsibility to his children to do all he can to make sure they don't repeat his mistakes. He can't make them accept Christ, but he can influence them—first by his own walk with God, and second by creating the environment that is conducive to the child's spiritual and moral development.

I realize that this is not easy. Many of the problems with our kids are due to the seeds we sowed for years. Some of our mistakes may be correctable, but in any case we must do whatever we can and pray that God will overrule our mistakes.

What about the spouse of a Transition Christian who won't accept Christ? I believe the Scriptures give us clear direction on this. Paul writes, "If any brother has a wife who is an unbeliever, and she consents to live with him, let him not send her away. And a woman who has an unbelieving husband, and he consents to live with her, let her not send her husband away" (1 Corinthians 7:12,13). Unfortunately, many times the unbelieving spouse *does* leave, and that produces pressure on the Transition Christian and on a church that is trying to minister to that person.

1. Samuel L. Blumenfeld, *N.E.A.: Trojan Horse in American Education* (Boise, Idaho: The Paradigm Company, 1984), p. 247.

5

THE SINGLES SCENE

"Bill, I've got to meet you for lunch!" The urgency in Bob's voice convinced me to change my plans and meet him.

Bob and Denise were close friends of mine. They had been married for 30 years and their children were grown. For 25 years they had operated a very successful business. The business had two divisions. Bob ran one, overseeing about 30 employees; Denise ran the other, with about 20 employees. They lived in an 18-room mansion and frequently had church groups over for parties and Bible studies.

After we ordered, Bob, in his typically direct manner, got right to the point. "I've fallen in love with this girl who works for me, and we want to move in together."

In my equally blunt manner I responded, "Bob, men your age don't fall in love; they fall in lust. You just want the nice firm flesh of a young girl next to you."

"No, this is the real thing!" he protested. He spoke glowingly about the young woman half his age who was one of his computer operators.

"You don't love this woman," I answered. "You have nothing to talk about. You're a businessman. She runs a computer. You have no friends in common, no interests in common. Nothing!" He was about to protest when I said, "Excuse me, you do have two things going for you. You have an interest in her firm young flesh, and she has an interest in your firm old wallet. Other than that you have absolutely nothing in common."

Bob was so infatuated that he couldn't hear my reasoning. A few days later Denise called. "Bob's moved out and filed for divorce," she said through her tears. "He rented an apartment in town and that girl has moved in with him." She poured out her grief, saying, "Bob doesn't know what he's doing. This girl doesn't love him. She urged him to file for the divorce, but I know her kind. She won't stay with him. She'll take him for all she can and then move on. He doesn't realize the destruction he's causing." I tried to comfort Denise as best I could, realizing there was very little I could do at this point besides listen.

In the 49 states where there are no-fault divorce laws, the moment someone files for divorce, the state recognizes that couple as divorced. So when Bob filed for divorce, the only issue to be decided was the division of property. The dissolution of the marriage was assumed. There was no waiting period, no attempt to produce reconciliation. The judge ruled that Denise could keep the house, and the business would be divided, with the details to be negotiated between their lawyers. Bob was so eager to speed the process along that much of the business went to Denise.

When the young woman saw how much of Bob's money was lost because of the divorce, and she realized that Bob was going to start a new business and it would take some time to build that business up, she was no longer interested in the relationship. Six months after the divorce she left for greener pastures.

Meanwhile, Denise was absolutely shattered. She no longer felt comfortable in the adult Bible study that she and her husband used to attend, so she moved over to the church's adult singles Bible study. But she missed her old friends, and she was lonely in her huge house. In her vulnerable condition she entered into a relationship with the first available man who was close to her age. With the blessing of her church she quickly remarried, but it soon became obvious that theirs was a very unhappy relationship.

About the time Denise remarried, Bob recognized the error of his ways and wanted to seek reconciliation. But it was too late. The legal process and the church itself had unwittingly conspired to end their marriage.

It's a tragedy that the church hasn't sought to change the no-fault divorce laws. One hundred years ago you could obtain a divorce only if your spouse had committed adultery—and that had to be proven in a court of law—or was insane or was guilty of a felony and was sentenced to prison. Today people can divorce for any frivolous reason. You cannot contest the divorce; you can only contest the property settlement and custody of children. There isn't even a cooling-off period to allow the partners to reevaluate.

I was only 22 years old when I went through my first divorce. It happened in Hawaii, and the judge ruled that there would be a one-year waiting period. The divorce would be final if there was no reconciliation during that year.

This is an important point: *The law allowed time to save a marriage.* It didn't save my marriage to Susan, but it might well have saved Bob and Denise's marriage. If there had been a waiting period, Bob would have moved out, had his fling, discovered the error of his ways, repented, and returned to his wife. The attorneys wouldn't have taken their 30 or 40 thousand dollars to try to sort through the mess. *This marriage ended because the system does not allow for people to make mistakes in judgment.*

I believe Christians ought to do everything possible to change these laws. Pressure needs to be put on state legislatures to change no-fault divorce laws. There are too many marriages failing that could be fixed with tougher laws, and those marriages should be saved for the good of the children and the health of our society.

Instead, what is the church's answer to this problem? Singles groups! A prominent church in Dallas runs a large ad in the TV Magazine section of the Sunday paper. It's conspicuously placed among ads for astrology readings, custom upholstery, abortion services, home remodeling, and legal assistance for bankruptcy, DWI, and misdemeanors. Here's what it says:

SINGLE?

Join the Club
Tired of Single's Bars, Pretentious
People, and Wasted Weekends?
Join the Club
Do You Appreciate Old-Fashioned

Values Like Honesty, Sincerity,
and Responsibility?
Join the Club
Can't Stand Phonies, Game-Players,
and The Night Club Crowd?
Join the Club
Ready To Meet Someone With Your
Interests, Attitudes, and Lifestyle?
FREE DATING BROCHURE
Christian Single Adults' Dating Service

Then there is a phone number to call—manned 24 hours a day—for more information. This church is not unique; I've seen similar ads all around the country.

What's so bad about that? you ask. Isn't this an outreach, a way to meet a pressing need in our society? No! Christians don't realize the message they are sending with such an ad. They are opening their fellowship to all kinds of people, some of whom have less-than-honorable motives. They are saying that singles aren't complete unless they're matched up with someone from the opposite sex. They are saying that it is more important to date than to address the deep spiritual needs that many singles have. Adult singles who are divorced need spiritual care rather than encouragement to match up again in a new, often disastrous relationship.

Take, for example, a woman who was my secretary. When I asked her how she had come to faith in Christ, she told me she had been divorced three times. She had tried a white-collar worker, a blue-collar worker, and a partier who drank too much. One day as she was driving in Dallas she passed a prominent Baptist church and this thought suddenly occurred to her: "I've never tried a Baptist husband. He'd have to be better than what I've had so far. Maybe I ought to start going to church and find a Baptist husband."

This woman was dead serious, and she proved it the following Sunday by dressing up in her most provocative dress and herding her kids into the car. Her sole purpose in attending church was to catch a man. Fortunately, in this case she got saved! There, you say, that proves that singles ministries are good, right? But the singles ministry had nothing to do with this woman's conversion. Her point in telling me this story was that she felt she was incomplete without a husband. When she met Christ and made Him the Lord and center of her life, she discovered she was complete. *She wasn't complete because of a husband; she was complete because of Jesus Christ.*

That's the issue we need to address regarding ministries to singles. The message that singles get in many churches—sometimes overt, often subtle—is that they're not a significant part of the church body unless they're married. Apart from the actual worship services, they generally cannot intermingle with married couples. In some cases they are actually told to go to the singles class. In one way or another singles get the message that they aren't welcome because they aren't attached.

Where does it say in Scripture that I am incomplete unless I have a husband or a wife? If I have Christ I have all I need. I don't expect that when I get to heaven God will tell me, "Bill, you really didn't need me. What you needed was a good wife." So why do many churches persist in segregating single adults from the mainstream of the congregation?

I had my eyes opened early in my Christian walk to the problems in this area. On my first Sunday in an adult singles class, there were two men and 12 women. The couple that led the class had been happily married for 20 years, and they welcomed me warmly. On the second Sunday a very attractive single woman named Charlotte introduced herself to me and said, "After I saw you last week, I really had it in my heart to pray for you."

"How nice," I thought. "I can use all the prayer I can get." I didn't think any more about it.

The following week Charlotte talked to me again and said, "I'm still praying about you."

"Thank you," I said. "I really appreciate that."

The next week the woman who taught the class called me. "Did you know that Charlotte is really praying about you?" she asked.

"She told me the same thing on Sunday. I appreciate it, but why is she doing that?"

"Well, you know . . . she's really praying *about* you."

"Excuse me, but what do you mean she's really praying about me?"

"You know. She's praying about you. Are you going to do anything about it?"

"Do *what* about it?"

There was an embarrassed moment of silence, as though it was so obvious that she shouldn't have to tell me. "Well . . . are you going to maybe take her somewhere . . . you know, maybe have dinner or something?"

Finally I got the message. *This girl was asking me for a date!* "Boy, am I dense!" I thought. There was a surge of anger, but I tried to control it as I explained my feelings to the Sunday school teacher. "Well, I'm really in the class to study the Bible. I don't have time to get involved in that kind of relationship. For one thing, I travel too much. And I've got other priorities, primarily learning about my faith. I hope you understand."

I don't think she did, for I got the distinct impression that her primary objective was to get everyone in the class married off. Apparently the other men felt that way too, for they rarely lasted in the class more than a month before moving on, usually to another church. I lasted six months.

I wish I could say that this type of experience is unique. Unfortunately, many singles have related similar stories. I believe that people who want to minister to singles are sincere, but most of them, if they've grown up in the church and enjoyed a happy Christian marriage, are ill-equipped to understand and minister to today's adults who find themselves "single again."

In another church singles group there was the ritual of the "secret pal." Each person in the class drew a number from a hat. Each number was matched to a name and you were supposed to send unsigned cards and letters to that individual for several weeks to encourage her and make her feel good about herself. Supposedly this was a random drawing directed by God, but in this case the Sunday school teacher helped God out by making sure that certain individuals were paired together. At the end of the quarter there was a party at a nice restaurant. Everyone brought a present and that's when you found out who was writing to you, when you were told who to give your present to.

I suppose the secret pal program isn't basically bad. But why did the teacher try to match us up with the "right" person? Why should I or any Christian have to go through such an experience? Why weren't these Sunday school teachers more concerned about my spiritual growth than running a Christian dating service? They didn't know my background. They didn't understand that I'd been through two disastrous marriages. They didn't realize the confusion I had, in which I often wondered whether I was even saved. I wanted to learn about the faith; they wanted to marry me off so I would fit into the mainstream of the church.

I even expressed this concern to a pastor once. I had just moved into a new community and started attending a church where I was told to attend the singles group. I told the pastor, "I do not believe adult singles should be placed in a situation where they feel different from the rest of the body. I feel that in order to be a part of the main body of this church, I will have to marry someone inside that singles group."

It was a rather awkward moment. "I think you misunderstand," he said. "You're not different from the rest of the body."

"Then why am I required to go to the singles class?"

"Well . . . you need to understand that it's rather awkward if singles are mixed with married couples. . . . It creates problems."

"Do you mean that a couple that's been married 20 years would feel threatened by my presence? Do you think that married women are in danger because I'm divorced? Are you afraid that some woman who's not happy in her marriage might get ideas because I'm divorced?"

"Bill, you don't understand. . . ."

Maybe he's right. I don't understand why just because some people are uncomfortable in a Sunday school class, they have to create a leper colony for divorced people. Isn't there some better way to handle the situation? Of course, it's taboo to mix your young singles who have never been married with the divorced singles. Parents who have raised their children in the church don't want their kids exposed to older singles who have learned the ways of the world. So we're isolated.

I wish I could say my experience was unusual and that most churches aren't like that. But I can't. As I've spoken around the country, many Transition Christians have related similar experiences. Single men especially feel they're pushed out of the church because it's a hunting ground for single women. If you're only interested in spiritual growth, the mating games can chase you away. Most of the rank-and-file membership of a church aren't even aware of this. How can they be? They rarely even meet the adult singles.

Often, divorced people end up going to churches that specialize in ministry to singles. I spoke to a large church in Minneapolis like that. It was made up entirely of single or remarried adults. Most of them were divorced and/or single parents. They came because they found in this church a giant support group that understood their needs. The church holds small group meetings for those coming out of bad relationships, much the way Alcoholics Anonymous conducts its open discussions. Individuals learn that they are not alone with their problems, and with that realization plus guided spiritual direction comes healing.

I'm glad there are churches like that, and many of them are doing a great work. But how much better it would be if all churches had the same concern. The church in America needs to recognize that we're increasingly becoming a singles-oriented society. According to futurist Alvin Toffler in his book *The Third Wave*, the traditional nuclear family of a working husband and a wife at home with two children is virtually obsolete. Only seven percent of homes fit that description.[1] Today one-fifth of all U.S. households consist of one person. According to the U.S. Census Bureau, 45 percent of all children born in 1978 will spend at least part of their childhoods with only one parent.[2] Of course, most of us realize that approximately 50 percent of all marriages end in divorce.

As single adults enter the church, they bring problems—baggage, as I called it earlier in the book. They're hurt by broken relationships. They may have endured physical or verbal abuse from a spouse. Perhaps they were victims of physical or sexual abuse as children, and saw the pattern repeated in their own families. Alcohol or drug abuse may have complicated their lives. The answer is not to segregate them until they find a new mate. The answer is to recognize these people are injured—spiritually injured. Their marriages need repairs. They need to try, for the sake of the children, to work out their problems and restore their families. But all too often that doesn't happen. It certainly didn't happen to me. And it didn't happen with Denise. Instead, we were placed in the Christian equivalent of a singles bar. We needed counseling and support, not a dating service.

Part of the problem with single adults who come into the church is that they only present one side—their side—of the family situation. "It was all my husband's fault," a divorced woman says. "My wife isn't a Christian, and that's why she's leaving me," says a separated husband. These people need to be asked some hard questions. "Was it really all your husband's fault? You didn't do anything this guy didn't like?" No, you both had problems. If a man says that his spouse isn't a Christian, that information is rarely checked. In some cases I've found that the spouse *is* a believer but doesn't know how to express it or else is confused by the terminology or experience of her partner.

A lot of questions need to be asked in love. "Where is your husband (or wife) now? Can you still talk to him? Do you have children? Do you pass the children back and forth? What are *you* doing to try to put this marriage back together? What are *you* doing to try to put the family back together? Has your husband accepted Christ? Will he come in for counseling? Can we go and talk with him?"

In most cases those hard questions never get asked. The Transition Christian's story is accepted as fact, and the underlying problems are rarely addressed. Then that person remarries and life becomes even more complicated. Now rather than two adults trying to work out their problems, there are frequently as many as six. When two divorced people marry, each partner brings a set of kids to the new home. Those kids have to spend time with both natural parents. If they want to take a family vacation, schedules have to be coordinated with the other two families. It becomes a huge maze of intermingled relationships.

So what should we do? I believe the church can have a significant ministry to adults who are divorced and who have just joined the church. They should *not* be placed in adult singles groups initially. It's an unspoken assumption that people in adult singles groups are spiritually fit and ready for marriage. That is not a valid assumption. If they've failed in one or more marriages, and they're new in the faith, what would qualify them for a successful relationship now? Instead, there needs to be a waiting period so that the church and the Transition Christian can get better acquainted. During that time the church needs to provide some kind of counseling. These people need to understand why their marriages failed, and to learn God's principles about marriage, so that if they do remarry they're prepared to make the new marriage work.

One tool that can really help is a confidential questionnaire that allows the new Christian to give the church his spiritual history. At one time a computer program company in California, called Church Growth, provided such a questionnaire. It was part of a much larger program to utilize the abilities of church members. There are others now that aren't so complex.

I compare this to a medical doctor who automatically requires each new patient to fill out a medical information form.

This gives the physician a history of the patient's past illnesses and any medications to which the patient may be allergic. The doctor doesn't do this in order to condemn the patient's past or refuse him treatment. He needs this information in order to best treat the patient's physical problems.

A spiritual medical questionnaire would ask some very important questions such as:

"When did you accept Christ?"

"Do you have doubts about your salvation—always, frequently, occasionally?"

"What are your spiritual gifts? If you don't know or aren't sure, would you like to talk about it with someone?"

"Were you abused physically, emotionally, or sexually as a child?"

"Have you ever had a problem of excessive use of alcohol? Are you presently under treatment for alcoholism? Are your family members also involved in counseling?"

"Have you ever been treated for substance abuse?"

"Have you ever been involved in any of the following: Homosexuality, lesbianism, . . .?"

The purpose of this questionnaire is not to collect dirt, but to find out how to minister to hurting people. Churches should gather this information for at least two reasons. First, if a person is struggling in an area, hiding it won't help solve the problem. The person needs counseling and support so he can see Christ gain the victory in that area. But second, if the person has seen Christ provide victory over a problem area, then he can be a tremendous source of encouragement and help to a new believer coming into the church who is struggling with that problem.

For example, I came into the church as a single parent. Within 18 months of my conversion my wife had left me and remarried. I was already a failure as a parent with my older daughter; I certainly didn't want to fail again. But I felt I was the only one who had that problem. I wanted to rear Jade in a Christian home, but I had very little knowledge about how to do that. If only there had been someone in the church who had been through similar struggles. Maybe he had learned how to trust God as a single father over several years, and he could encourage me and counsel me. Or perhaps there were one or two other fathers in similar circumstances. If we could have met together with the aid of an experienced counselor, we could have helped each other work through our problems. My subsequent experience in hundreds of churches tells me that such men were probably in my congregation. Unfortunately, I never found out who they were, and most churches have no way of making such matches between needy people.

For a really large church with adequate financial resources such a questionnaire could be put on computer; the software is available. Then suppose a man comes into the pastor's office for counseling. He's 35 years old and homosexual. It's destroyed his marriage. The pastor can turn to his computer terminal, type in the pertinent information, and immediately get the name and number of one or more men who have experience and are qualified to minister in this area. Imagine the ministry possibilities! For those churches that can't afford such a system, there are smaller computer systems and even card-file systems that use a simpler questionnaire.

What's tragic is that most churches have the resources to help the Transition Christian in very practical ways but can't give that help because they're unaware of the resources available right within their own body. Even smaller congregations have more resources than they often realize. Once after a church service I was talking with an usher who told me that he had a lot of experience manufacturing various kinds of sports equipment. Later that morning as I was talking to the pastor he told me they were about ready to go out for bids to construct a basketball court behind the church.

"Pastor, I don't think you need to bid that out. The usher over there"—I pointed him out—"has experience in that area. Why don't you talk to him and see if he can't help you?" The pastor was amazed to learn that someone in his congregation was knowledgeable in that area. He just didn't know that this resource was available. If such situations exist in these practical areas, they exist even more in spiritual areas.

We've talked about what the *church* can do, but what about the Transition Christian who wants help but isn't getting it? If the Sunday school teacher isn't sensitive to his needs, or if he doesn't have anyone to support him in his problem area, where can he go? What I had to realize was that *I, not the church, am responsible for my own spiritual growth.* I had to accept responsibility for my own problems. I needed to aggressively seek God through prayer and Bible study and related reading to find the answers I needed. And if I needed counseling or support, it was my responsibility to search out that help.

If your needs aren't being met in your church, I strongly urge you to go to the pastor, tell him your situation, and ask him for advice about where to go to have your needs met. Do you need support with a Christian emphasis from a group of formerly married? Tell the pastor. Maybe he can match you with someone who can help. If he can't, ask him if there is a church or a ministry in the community that can address that need. I think most pastors would rather have people go where they belong than remain in their own church when they don't fit.

Even if you met Christ in that church, don't stay if your needs aren't being met. I'm not talking about church-hopping because you don't like the way the preacher talks or they don't play your kind of music. I'm talking about *essential areas of life.* If you're recently divorced and you sense that there's too much pressure to remarry and you feel that it's more important to grow in the faith, then go to a place where you can grow spiritually.

This applies to other areas of life as well. If you've had a drug problem but no one else in your church has had such a problem, and you're afraid you might go back to drugs, then you need to go where there's help—and fast!

1. Alvin Toffler, "The Family of the Future," in *Families*, Fall 1980, p. 67.
2. "The American Family: Bent—But Not Broken," in *U.S. News and World Report*, June 16, 1980, p. 48.

6

THE BENEFITS OF REMEMBERING THE PAIN

If you go to a church with 500 or more members, I can guarantee that someone in your congregation has a problem with substance abuse.

Surprised? Imagine what the Transition Christian who is a recovering alcoholic or drug-user thinks. The last thing he expects to find inside a church is an active alcoholic or drug-user. The church may not recognize the signs, but he sure does.

We shouldn't be shocked at such news. The church is made up of people, and they are not immune from the pressures of society. And in our society one out of every five Americans is affected directly by the problem of alcoholism. The fact that the church doesn't expect its members to have an addiction doesn't mean that there aren't weak brothers and sisters who have fallen and don't know where to find help. And even if there aren't any members who are addicted, there will inevitably be members who are hurting because a close relative has an addiction problem.

Two examples will illustrate how insidious the problem is. I was speaking in a church where the pastor's wife was almost paranoid about having ex-alcoholics or drug-users in the congregation. She was afraid of the negative impact they might have on the youth. Yet the minute I met her I knew she was on something; she had all the signs of a person hooked on amphetamines. Most prominent were the intricate flowers and birds that she had painted on her fingernails. This is a popular pastime of a person on amphetamines.

I took the pastor aside and asked him, "Does your wife take

any pills for a diet problem or something like that?"

"Yes, she does," he said. "But it's only a limited amount and she gets them through our family doctor."

"Please don't be offended by what I'm about to say, but as a reformed alcoholic and someone who's worked with many substance-abusers, I think your wife has a serious problem. I'd strongly recommend that you dig a little deeper. For the sake of your family, check it out."

Fortunately, this pastor took my advice. He called the family doctor to find out what he had prescribed. He checked in his wife's medicine cabinet and discovered that the names of three doctors were on the bottles. He called the other two doctors and discovered that they had issued the same prescriptions to his wife. She was taking many times the number of pills prescribed. When confronted, she admitted her problem. She said that every time she tried to reduce the number of pills, she went into withdrawal symptoms.

Let me quickly say that the overwhelming majority of people inside the church do not have an addiction problem. But we mustn't let that blind us to the fact that all of us are human and some of us are susceptible to substance abuse. And it may not be the obvious substances that we automatically condemn— alcohol and hard drugs. There are substances that are considered acceptable that can be equally addictive, such as diet pills or sugar. These substances may not cause serious social problems and so may be overlooked. But don't think they aren't habit-forming.

The second example was one that I didn't recognize right away, though I should have. Perhaps I didn't want to see the evidence. The man had just graduated from Bible school and was working for my ministry. Within 30 days I noticed several classic outward signs of problem drinking. When I would call him at night his voice would be louder than normal, and occasionally he was almost incoherent. His wife was constantly nervous about him. If he was five minutes late arriving home, she would call the office. He was constantly telling me not to come too close to him—"I think I'm getting a terrible cold and

I don't want you to catch it." The primary signal that I should have recognized was the huge bottle of mouthwash in his car.

One evening I swung by his house to leave some work and noticed that his screen door had a hole punched in it toward the street. I asked him about it and he said, "Oh, someone tried to break into the house." I thought to myself, "That's strange. If someone was breaking into the house, the screen would have been pushed in rather than out."

Finally I determined that I had to confront him, but the newspapers beat me to it. A short article reported that this man had been indicted for fraud. Apparently during his Bible school years he had sold some products which he never delivered. He had pocketed people's money to support his habit. The story also revealed that he had twice been arrested for drunk driving while he was a student. The man called me that morning to offer his resignation.

This man's pattern was typical. He had become a smooth liar to cover up his drinking habit. His wife was nervous because she was always concerned that he was off drinking somewhere and might have an accident while driving home. In fact, she had a well-paying job of her own to make sure the family had enough money to feed the kids and pay the rent. I didn't recognize the signs initially because I didn't want to admit that this handsome, personable young man with so much potential might have a problem.

The fact is that the Christian who has a problem with alcohol or some other substance is highly motivated to hide his problem. He shows up at church on Sunday smiling, with teeth brushed and mouth fresh, and looks and acts the role of a good Christian. His problem is hidden to all but his family. The Transition Christian comes into the church trying to overcome an addiction problem. He needs some kind of support group, but he doesn't find it. In fact he is told that the problem doesn't exist inside the church. But because of his experience he sees evidence of problems. What does he do in such a situation?

I know one reformed drug-user who went to his pastor and said, "I think you have a problem with some of your teenagers. I was a drug-user once, and I see all the signs that some of your kids are using drugs."

The pastor absolutely denied it. "No, that's not true of *our* church. I know our kids, and none of them would ever use drugs." This pastor simply refused to recognize the signals.

The struggle which the Transition Christian faces coming out of substance-abuse is that the church has difficulty distinguishing between the spiritual problem and the physical problem. He started taking alcohol or drugs initially because he had a spiritual problem. Now he's accepted Christ and the spiritual problem is being addressed. But because of the drug's effect on his body, he now has a physical problem as well. In most cases that physical problem doesn't disappear just because the spiritual problem is solved.

For example, how many pastors know that the best thing you can do for an alcoholic during the first 24 hours when he's trying to come off alcohol is feed him candy bars and honey? That's because there's a huge amount of sugar in hard booze— a pound or more in a fifth of bourbon. So the alcoholic is accustomed to all those carbohydrates and sugar pouring into his body. His body actually craves sugar as much as it craves alcohol.

How many Christians realize that there's a cycle which the typical abuser goes through? The further away from his past he gets, the more likely he is to slip back into his habit. And sometimes it's the spouse that actually causes that reversal.

The substance-abuser's problems aren't just physical. There are problems that arise in his family. Suppose the man of the house has had a drinking problem. His wife has had to take control of the house. She takes a good-paying job and makes sure the bills are paid. She makes all the financial decisions. The kids come to her, not Dad, with their problems. She is in charge. Then the alcoholic comes to his senses. Perhaps he is told that he will lose his job if he doesn't shape up. Maybe his wife packs up the kids and goes home to her mother. He goes to a church and the pastor leads this man to Christ. He sobers up and starts attending church. He persuades his wife and family to come back and he starts fulfilling his responsibility in the home.

This new situation predictably causes major conflict. The family has learned to function without the man of the house. Now he wants to make decisions about their finances. The children begin to go to him with their problems. The wife is no longer the sole authority and she doesn't know how to handle that change. Without consciously realizing it, she begins to sabotage his recovery.

It happens so innocently. Husband and wife are at a nice restaurant. The wife says something like, "Honey, you've been so good. You haven't had a drink in six months. Why don't we celebrate? You deserve a glass of wine." That glass of wine starts him on a downward spiral. Soon it's a six-pack of beer. Then a few days later it happens—he goes out and gets dead drunk. He wakes up the next morning distraught. He goes to his pastor and says, "I don't know what happened." The pastor thinks it's a spiritual problem, that he's not right with God. Neither of them recognize that at least part of the problem is the man's wife.

You see, no one warned this family that there were going to be changes, and that those changes would be traumatic. If the man had gone to Alcoholics Anonymous, they would have told him to have his wife go to an Alanon meeting. And the first thing they would have told her at that meeting was, "You're in for big trouble. Your husband is going to sober up and he's going to take the home away from you. He's going to get the respect back from his kids. They're going to start going to him with their problems instead of you. He's going to take the checkbook away and start paying the bills, probably within the next three months." This woman would have been prepared. Instead, the church only addressed the man's spiritual problem and thought that solved it all.

Recently I talked with a man whose son had used all sorts of drugs. In order to support his habit, the boy had stolen his father blind. He had stolen credit cards, stolen checks, and forged his father's signature, stolen the stereo out of the front room, and wrecked the father's car. "One night he stole my Rolex watch," the man said. "That watch cost me 5000 dollars, and he pawned it for 500 dollars!

"Then wouldn't you know it—one night my son comes home and tells me, 'Dad, I met Jesus.' 'Sure,' I told him. 'And what kind of drugs were you using when you met Jesus? Uppers? Downers? What kind of brain damage do you have? Was this Jesus black or white? Are you sure you didn't meet Krishna?' "

This man was angry, and can you blame him? He wasn't going to be impressed with his son's conversion until he saw some evidence of genuine repentance. The son was going to church and getting help from his peers, but who was going to deal with the dad? Someone from the church needed to call on that father and say, "Your son has had a real experience with Christ. He really has stopped taking drugs and he wants to straighten out his life. Would you come down and talk to some other parents whose children have also been on drugs?"

That man needs to deal with his anger, and one of the ways to help him is to arrange for him to meet other fathers who have had similar experiences. Then he will realize that he's not alone. As he hears other men tell about how Christ has changed their lives, this man will learn that there is hope. His son can change, and *he* can change too.

The problem of the woman alcoholic is equally challenging. We're talking about the family where the wife and mother is an alcoholic who has lived on carbohydrates, mostly starchy macaroni dishes. There is no meat in their meals because she has stolen food money for her booze. However, the budget for cooking wine is unbelievable. But only very little of that wine goes into the food. Most housewives with a drinking problem drink from the moment they get up, then hide their alcohol before the husband comes home. Their drinking pattern is the reverse of most men. Most pastors don't understand this.

I believe that there's one very simple but crucial solution that the church ought to consider. Invite groups such as Alcoholics Anonymous, Palmer Drug Abuse Program (PDAP), Alanon, Alateen, and other support groups to hold their meetings in church facilities. These groups have proven their effectiveness over the years. They don't have all the answers, but they have a lot of them, and the answers they do have can motivate people to seek a deeper relationship with Jesus Christ.

Unfortunately, I know of few fundamental, evangelical churches that are willing to allow such groups to meet on their premises. And that's a tragedy. It's true that AA doesn't lead people to Jesus Christ, but without AA I might never have made the connection with Christ. If they had told me in that first meeting that I had to place my life in the hands of Jesus Christ in order to stop drinking, I probably would have left that night and started drinking again. But they said, "You have to turn your life over to the care of God as you understand him. So you don't believe in a real God? Then pick that chair. At least it can stand on its feet and you can't."

What I found was that AA took me to a certain level of recovery, to a realization that I needed God and His help if I was to have victory. Gradually I realized that this wasn't enough. I found I needed the Person of Jesus Christ.

In my case I wasn't ready to hear about Jesus Christ when I attended my first AA meeting. If they had told me I had to accept Jesus Christ in order to be freed from alcohol, I would have left the meeting. A bridge needed to be built. We do the same thing in our ministry at atheist conventions. I never try to convince an atheist that Jesus Christ is God. Never. The reason is simple: You don't argue over the name of God when the individual doesn't believe in God. *First* you convince him that there is a God, *then* you tell him His name.

Many recovering alcoholics have the same realization I had. There comes a point where an individual has to complete his spiritual experience. He needs Jesus Christ. And where will he meet Christ? Well, if the group is meeting in the church, isn't it natural to think that at least some members of AA might begin thinking, "AA is talking about trusting God . . . they worship God at this church . . . it's a nice-looking place . . . maybe this God we're talking about has a name . . . I ought to come back on Sunday and learn His name."

That's exactly what happens at Grace Community Church in Tempe, Arizona. It's one of the few evangelical churches I know which has support-group meetings for alcoholics and drug-abusers in their facilities. Many, many rehabilitated individuals are now a part of their church as a result. The church, under the leadership of Pastor Guy Davidson, has also established support groups for people with other emotional problems.

Most churches that allow AA meetings are of the more liberal persuasion. The Catholic Church has an alternative to AA called Alcoholics Victorious. The only difference is that instead of knowing God as you understand Him, they substitute Jesus Christ. Of course they get few nonbelievers. The organization is geared for practicing Catholics who are also practicing alcoholics.

Allowing AA and other groups to meet at church has another benefit: It allows concerned church members to visit the meetings to better understand the needs of people they desire to reach. And perhaps even more important, it announces to the congregation that if someone has a problem with substance abuse, there's a place for him or her to go for help—right there within the church.

If this seems so logical, then why aren't more churches doing it, or at least providing some kind of Christian alternative? I think I know why, but I don't like it. Most people who are addicted to alcohol or a drug are also addicted to other things. They have an addictive personality. I was talking with a stewardess on American Airlines during a long flight. I observed that when I walk to the back of an airplane, the number of drinks seemed to increase in the smoking section. She agreed: "The smoking section of the plane takes up about 20 percent of the sets. But we sell twice as much alcohol in the smoking section as the nonsmoking section."

A vast majority of people at AA meetings smoke. The language is pretty rough. They drink a lot of coffee—in fact, they're often addicted to caffeine. (When I was drinking, I got high in the morning by drinking coffee, then came back down drinking alcohol.) They have spiritual, mental, and physical problems because of their habit. They sure don't talk like Mary Poppins. Their conversation is often filled with sexual innuendos. I was at a PDAP meeting once where a teenage girl confessed, "I banged five guys in one night." Now that's not the kind of talk we like to hear around our church halls. Just imagine if one of our kids from the Sunday school heard that!

These people may have stopped drinking, but as is sometimes said, "When you sober up a drunken SOB, you have a sober SOB." Unless the spiritual problem is solved, nothing's changed except that the person doesn't drink now. He's the same rotten individual he was before—and he's desperately in need of Christ. If he's meeting in the church building, isn't there a greater chance of him meeting Christ? Of course someone will raise this issue: Suppose one of those ex-alcoholics goes off the wagon and has a key to the church and comes in and steals the sound system. It's true, there is a risk. That's why we have insurance! Aren't the potential ministry results worth some risk?

In addition to having AA and similar meetings in the church, I think seminaries ought to invite such groups to use their facilities, or else seminarians ought to be required to attend some meetings of AA or PDAP. Many pastors learn all about ministry in seminary, but they have little preparation for ministry in real-life situations. It's like a medical student learning all about disease in medical school, but if he never has an internship where he goes into the hospital and sees firsthand the diseases he's studying, how will he be prepared to treat them after he graduates?

Pastors need to learn what sin is. It's not an abstract concept; it's something people do. Ministers need to learn how to deal with the 50-year-old man who's finally off booze after 30 years but can't shake the smoking habit. They need to witness the agony of a young woman who's going through withdrawal from heroin addiction. They need to sit and listen in a PDAP group when one of the members is forced to stop making excuses and face up to his problems. It's not pretty, but that's real life.

I'm so glad that Dr. Anderson Spickard came out with his book for Christians called *Dying for a Drink* (Word, 1985). Dr. Spickard is Director of General Internal Medicine and Professor of Medicine at Vanderbilt University Medical Center. He admits that he once held to the belief that addiction was strictly a spiritual problem.

> The implication is that addiction is strictly a spiritual problem and that alcoholics and drug addicts who give themselves to God and faithfully attend church services and Bible studies will be cured of the problem.
>
> I identify deeply with this point of view because it was once my own, and I know it often springs from a deep concern and compassion for addicted people. At the same time, I have learned from painful experience that the search for a "Christian" solution to the problem of addiction usually does more harm than good, and in a sad number of cases it prevents alcoholics from getting the help they need.[1]

Dr. Spickard claims that the church inadvertently encourages the alcoholic in his addiction by failing to recognize the medical severity of his problem. "Drinking is too often seen as a minor symptom of sin rather than an uncontrollable habit that can kill."[2] That's why the church needs to team up with proven programs like AA and medical programs for the more serious cases. After treatment, the church can become an important focal point in the recovery process.

There is another danger that is very real in the church. The longer the recovering addict is in the church and removed from his habit, the easier it is to forget how bad his problem really was. And when that happens, look out!

I know a man who was once the worst drunk his town had ever known. Twenty years after he was miraculously saved, stories of his drinking were still told around town. But to hear him talk today, you'd think that the only answer to the problem of alcoholism is punishment. I was sitting with him and his pastor in a restaurant when he said, "All those drunk drivers should be thrown in jail and they ought to throw the keys away."

What a tragic perspective! This man forgot that 20 years earlier he had been jailed several times for drunkenness. If they had thrown away the key, he wouldn't be sitting in this nice restaurant right now. This man could have a significant ministry to alcoholics . . . if he would only remember how bad off he once was!

Even more dangerous is the fact that when you don't remember how bad it was, it's easier to slip back into the addiction. A man I knew woke up one morning and walked out to his garage and found that his car was gone. After a moment of panic he found his car parked in front of the house, and he wondered why he had parked there—something he never did. He walked out and discovered that the fender was bent and that something red was on the bumper. Suddenly he realized that he didn't remember driving home the previous night. Obviously he must have hit something on the way home, and he probably had parked the car out front so his wife wouldn't see the car when she left for work. But he didn't know what he had hit—or who! Was that red paint on his bumper? Or blood?

That shock immediately sobered the man up. He checked the newspapers and called all the area hospitals to try to find out if there was an unsolved hit-and-run case. When he didn't find anything he concluded, "Thank God I didn't kill anybody." He had his car fixed, and for the next three months he didn't drink a drop of alcohol. But he didn't go to Alcoholics Anonymous or church, either. And gradually the memory of that throat-choking moment faded. He even rationalized that he had just sideswiped a red car, and it really hadn't been that bad. Finally he gave himself permission to drink again, promising, "I won't drink so much now, so I can always remember where I've been and what I've done."

On the first night he went out to his favorite bar he got drunk. While driving home he hit a kid on a bicycle and killed him. The man didn't learn about it until the next day, when the police came to his home and arrested him. He was convicted of manslaughter and sent to prison, where he finally got involved in AA.

Every night that story is repeated in this country. Are Transition Christians immune? Will a former substance abuser who has met Christ stay clean just because he's a Christian? I wish that were true.

One evening I was passing through Atlanta and had a layover between flights. As usual, I dropped in at the Crown Room to make some phone calls, and there in one corner lay an old friend of mine, passed out on the couch. The aroma of alcohol was obvious within five feet of him. This man had once been a famous evangelist who traveled all over the country. Many people met Christ because of his preaching. I went over and shook him to see if I could wake him up and help him in some way. But it was useless; he was out cold.

I thought of the dramatic testimony he had had for years. As a young man he was a salesman who took his large paychecks on Friday and spent them almost entirely on alcohol. One night he woke up to find himself lying in six inches of water in a gutter. The water had actually lapped into his mouth and he had nearly drowned. He had stumbled to his feet and wandered into a gospel mission and met Christ. Almost immediately he left his job and entered Bible school, and within four years he was an evangelist.

I don't know where the first slippage occurred. I think it probably happened at a dinner with some prestigious people where it was expected that all the guests would have wine with their meal. I do remember that I was surprised the first time I saw him drinking wine, knowing his background as an alcoholic. The next time I saw him he was drinking bourbon and Coke. The next time he was drinking straight bourbon. The next time I saw him was in the Crown Room at the Atlanta Airport, and his ministry was completely shut down.

From the moment this evangelist took his first glass of wine until his ministry was destroyed took less than a year. Toward the end he had preached that a little bit of anything won't hurt; but a whole lot of something had sure hurt him! He had claimed total victory over alcohol, but he had forgotten one of the major tenets of AA: We claim victory one day at a time. It's no different as Christians: Every day we need to be filled with the Holy Spirit. We can't rely on what the Spirit did yesterday to provide what we need for today.

To think it started so innocently. How could one glass of wine make that much difference? Why did he even take that glass of wine? There are no easy answers, but I think one crucial factor is that this evangelist forgot how bad it really was. He forgot what it felt like to wake up in the middle of that gutter. He thought he could handle one glass of wine now. But he couldn't.

That's the problem many Christians have. We are told to forget our past and press on to the prize of knowing Christ. I agree that we are to press on. I agree that we are to meditate about the fact that Christ has saved us. *But we cannot just remember that we've been saved; we must also remember what Christ has saved us from.* We need to remember sin in all its ugly horror, and remember that Christ *rescued* us from it.

Frankly, that's the strength of AA, PDAP, and other treatment programs. Just when you begin to think it wasn't so bad after all, you hear a fresh testimony to remind you that it really was that bad. Even when a person has been sober for 20 years, if he goes to AA he'll meet someone who has just come in off the street to tell how he couldn't find his car and he can't remember how he got home the other night. The person listening will shake his head and remember—that was me 20 years ago!

God knows the power of this truth, for the Scriptures are filled with examples of the sin of men. Why do you think the Israelites were constantly reminded that God had saved them from the horrors of Egypt? Because they forgot how bad slavery was and how hard they had to work and how brutally they were treated. Look at this warning in Deuteronomy 6:

> It shall come about when the Lord your God brings you into the land which He swore to your fathers, Abraham, Isaac and Jacob, to give you, great and splendid cities which you did not build, and houses full of all good things which you did not fill, and hewn cisterns which you did not dig, vineyards and olive trees which you did not plant, and you shall eat and be satisfied, *then watch yourself, lest you forget the Lord who brought you from the land of Egypt, out of the house of slavery* (Deuteronomy 6:10-12).

All through the Old Testament we read of how Israel experienced God's blessing, then strayed and worshiped other Gods. At that point God judged them, usually by bringing in an invading army that hauled them off into captivity. Then the people would repent and God would restore their freedom. A few years would pass and the people would forget again, and the whole pattern would be repeated.

The apostle Paul often contrasts the old man and the new man. He reminds us that once we carried out the desires of the flesh, but now we are to walk in the power of the Holy Spirit:

> Therefore consider the members of your earthly body as dead to immorality, impurity, passion, evil desire, and greed, which amounts to idolatry. For it is on account of these things that the wrath of God will come, *and in them you also once walked*, when you were living in them. But now you also, put them all aside: anger, wrath, malice, slander, and abusive speech from your mouth (Colossians 3:5-8).

I could give many examples. The point is that while the church must welcome the Transition Christian with open arms, it should never advise him to forget his past. That was one of my benefits in writing my first book, *My Life Without God*. Frankly, I hated writing that book because it dredged up so many painful memories that I would rather not remember. But those very memories keep me from going back. When I recall the hell of my life without God, I don't want to go back. It motivates me to thank God for the wonderful gift of salvation He has given me.

Let's never take that gift lightly.

1. Anderson Spickard, Jr., and Barbara Thompson, "Dying for a Drink," in *Christianity Today*, May 17, 1985, p. 26.
2. Terry Muck, " 'Enabler' or Positive Force?" Book review in *Christianity Today*, May 17, 1985, p. 77.

7

SIN TAKES TIME

I was in San Francisco to reach out to delegates and their families who were participating in the annual American Atheists Convention organized by my mother. Part of the team that helped me in the extensive street witnessing we did around the convention hotel was called SOS, short for "Streets of San Francisco." They are a group of former homosexuals that have accepted Jesus Christ as their Lord and abandoned their homosexual lifestyle, and are now aggressively reaching out to that subculture in the bay area.

In return for helping me, they asked me to speak one night at a street meeting in the Tenderloin District, the heart of the city's homosexual activity. So on Friday night at about 10:00 I walked into that area to meet the group at the designated location. A block from my destination a young man stopped me and asked, "Aren't you Bill Murray?" I acknowledged that I was. "I saw your picture in the paper and then I saw you with the SOS people today. Could I talk to you for a minute?"

We stepped into a doorway off the sidewalk so he could have some privacy. "I was saved out of homosexuality," he told me.

"Well, great. Praise God!" I said.

The man dropped his eyes and stared at the pavement. "Well, not really."

"What do you mean?"

He heaved a great sigh and said, "I was involved in SOS for two years. But about three months ago . . . I fell back into the homosexual scene. I'm ashamed to go back to SOS." He started to cry. "Will you pray for me? I want to go back, but . . ."

I was moved by the man's confession and we had a time of prayer. Then I escorted him over to some of the SOS group who recognized him and welcomed him with open arms. Immediately he started passing out tracts on the street.

What happened next was frightening. We were surrounded by members of a group called the Gay Revolutionary Socialist Front. As we handed out material and talked to passersby, they jeered us and spit on us. Whenever someone talked with us they would mock, "Oh, look at that! They got another sinner for Christ!"

The young man with whom I had just prayed took the worst abuse. Two of the group went right up to him and shouted, "Look what we have here! We had this kid last night, and now here he is back with SOS! What's the matter? Didn't you like us?" That young man went through hell in order to return to Christ's fold.

Later that night, after our street meeting, I talked with some of the SOS people about our evening and reflected on what had happened to that young man. Never having experienced the homosexual drive, I had naively thought that once a homosexual was saved, he was forever freed from homosexuality. It never occurred to me that a Christian could slip back into that lifestyle.

Of course, if I had thought about how Christians struggle in other areas of sin, I would have realized that the sexual area is no different. Satan knows our weaknesses, and he sure knew how to trip up that young man. When that man stumbled he wondered, like many of us, if he was truly saved and if he could ever be forgiven.

I learned that this man had worked for two years within the SOS and that during this time he had been straight. But after two years he hadn't married, nor had he truly redirected his sexual urge. Through years of orgasmic activity he had programmed his hormonal drive. The tug-of-war within was powerful, and he was unable to redirect it.

This battle is one that many of us have a hard time understanding. As a homosexual, sex is easy. It can be had anytime, day or night, without building a relationship. In fact, the average "gay" has sex with 500 or more different partners during his lifetime! This is vastly different from God's design for sex. Not only does God deplore homosexuality, but His plan for men and women is that sex is to occur within the confines of marriage.

Why did this SOS member revert back to his old lifestyle? Probably because he was used to "cheap sex." The Christian standard is to build a relationship with a woman and to marry, or else to have no sex at all. For whatever reasons, he found both difficult. My friends within SOS speculated that one day when he was vulnerable he found himself in the wrong place at the wrong time. Perhaps he met another young man who gave him a warm smile and said, "Gee, I'd like to make you feel good tonight," and in that moment he caved in. Then he was ashamed. He felt like he had committed the unpardonable sin. He concluded that he could never go back to his Christian friends after this. This man needed to be reminded that "if we confess our sins, He is faithful and righteous to forgive us our sins and to cleanse us from all unrighteousness" (1 John 1:9).

The area of sexual sin is so difficult for Christians to face. We're nervous about it. We don't want to talk about it, and we hope it won't affect our congregation. But our society doesn't ignore it. Illicit sex is glamorized in the media and even Christians cannot resist its lure. The Center for Population Options estimates that the average television viewer sees more than 9000 scenes of suggested sexual intercourse, sexual comment, or sexual innuendo each year![1] It's not surprising that more than half of all teenagers have already had sexual intercourse by the time they reach the age of 17. Many colleges are providing "safe sex kits" for any students who want them. The kit at Dartmouth College in New Hampshire includes a brochure called *Safe Sex* that describes options for "enjoying sex to the fullest without giving or getting sexual diseases."[2]

With unrestrained sexual activity not just accepted but actively promoted, many Christians—and not just Transition Christians—are fighting a losing battle. Rather than supporting each other, the church frequently ignores the societal pressures or issues blanket condemnations so that members tend to suffer their temptations privately.

Transition Christians coming out of sexual sin often find that they are not welcome in many churches. Members of SOS have literally formed their own church because they do not feel welcome in most evangelical churches in San Francisco. It goes without saying that most churches feel equally uncomfortable having them in their fellowship. It is so hard to look past the outward behavior! It is hard to be patient and allow God time to change them.

The same is true of ex-prostitutes or sexual deviants. They have a style of dress and a lingo that isn't appreciated inside the church. As with the gays, those things don't change overnight. Such outer habits are repulsive to many lifelong Christians who have difficulty looking deeper, to the work that God is doing inside these people. So they feel locked out of the very community which they need in order to experience total healing.

In addition, the church today faces an incredibly new opportunity for ministry with the AIDS epidemic. Already an estimated 1.5 million Americans are infected with the AIDS virus, and 90 percent of them don't even know it! A majority of them may eventually display the symptoms that lead to a slow, agonizing death. The church can react in horror to these people and shut them out, or else it can recognize the potential it has to demonstrate God's love to people who have no other hope.

When I think of how Christ welcomed the prostitute and other social outcasts into His kingdom, and how He reached out and touched society's untouchables—the lepers—I believe that He was setting an example for us today. People are discovering that the sexual revolution has not produced the fulfillment they expected. Old values are being rediscovered. Monogamy is again becoming a respected option. What group is better qualified to actively and positively lead the way than the church?

Many Transition Christians who enter the church are trying to leave behind a wholly hedonistic, promiscuous lifestyle. Sometimes the best thing for these new Christians is to temporarily put them in a separate setting away from their old lifestyle and away from the church. A 19-year-old prostitute received Christ at a crusade I conducted in Florida. Shortly after her conversion, our ministry sponsored her so she could attend a summer Bible camp in New York. There she was able to concentrate for hours each day learning about her new-found faith.

This woman wrote to me after she had been in camp just two weeks. She told me that the camp had communal showers for the girls. She didn't understand why, but she felt embarrassed when she was naked in front of the other girls in that shower area. "Isn't it funny," she wrote. "I used to be a prostitute and now I'm embarrassed when my body is naked." She didn't realize it, but Christ was taking her through a healing process so that she would not readily slip back into her former lifestyle. If she was going to be embarrassed taking off her clothes around women, then the odds of her returning to prostitution were negligible.

The point is that we must provide an environment for these people to grow. *There must be spiritual development beyond the fact that they have given up their old lifestyle.* These people don't need to be constantly reminded that their old sexual practices were wrong; they need to *replace* them with a godly lifestyle. When you've spent several hours every day in a particular activity for months or even years and now it's gone, that time must be filled with something else, or the sinner is in danger of return-ing to his old lifestyle.

Christ gave this parable to the Pharisees, and I think it applies to our discussion: "When the unclean spirit goes out of a man, it passes through waterless places, seeking rest, and does not find it. Then it says, 'I will return to my house from which I came;' and when it comes, it finds it *unoccupied*, swept, and put in order. Then it goes, and takes along with it seven other spirits more wicked than itself, and they go in and live there" (Matthew 12:43-45). I believe this passage illustrates the fact that we can't just remove sin from our lives; we must *replace* it with the life of Christ.

We cannot minimize the power of sex in our culture. Even though I come out of a totally humanistic background, I am till shocked at times by the power that sex has on people. At that same atheist convention in San Francisco I talked with a woman who bluntly informed me, "There is nothing except orgasm in life. That's all there is. So I make love to my husband in the morning. Then later in the morning I pick up a man and make love with him. Then I find another man in the afternoon, and I make love to my husband again when he comes home at night. I can't live without orgasm." Then she opened her purse and pulled out a nightgown. "See, I'm always prepared. Do you want to see how I look in my nightgown?"

I wasn't about to let that conversation go any further. I told her I wasn't interested and she moved on into the atheist convention. And why do you think she was attending that convention? Because atheism gave her the approval she needed to be involved in all her adultery. If she could convince herself that there was no God, then anything was okay. In fact, she told me she had had numerous abortions—she had even done some of them herself. If there is no God, then there are no moral absolutes.

Perhaps no area of morals is more affected in our generation than in this sexual area. There are people who spend every night of the week frequenting "meat markets." These are bars where the sole purpose of going is to meet someone with whom you can have sex that night. There is little entertainment, little drinking, and a stiff cover charge at the door.

For someone who has to have sex, it takes a lot of time to satisfy that drive. It takes time to get dressed up, go down to the meat market, find a new partner, then find a hotel or some other place to go. Of course, that's not just true for sex, it's true for any sin. *Sin takes time*. It not only takes time, *it feels good*. We enjoy it so much that we rarely think of its consequences.

Of course, no one starts out having sex four or five times a day. And a homosexual rarely begins his lifestyle in the Tenderloin District. Sin starts simply. That woman I met at the atheists' convention probably had her first sexual experience as a teenager. She enjoyed it and gradually got more deeply involved. Over the years she so programmed herself to look for sex that now it consumed her life.

That's how sin is—it's addicting. One glass of wine doesn't work with an alcoholic. One joint of marijuana doesn't satisfy a drug addict. Anyone who fulfills a sinful desire once is likely to do it again unless the habit is broken. There's no such thing as a one-time rapist. There's no such thing as a one-time shoplifter. In our society, with the way our system of law enforcement operates, you usually have to do something dozens of times before you're punished. If a young boy gets caught shoplifting, more than likely he has shoplifted 20 times before he got caught. A drunk driver is normally arrested once for every 100 times he drives drunk. Nothing prevented these people from continuing their habits, so when they got caught, their habits were firmly ingrained.

I once had a secretary who stole a thousand dollars from me. She counted the cash I brought back from crusade offerings and deposited the money in the bank. When she altered the deposit slip and kept the thousand dollars, I caught the discrepancy. I asked her pastor to meet with us, and at first the woman denied the charge. But the evidence was so great that she finally confessed, and then said this was the first time she had ever stolen anything.

"That's very difficult for me to believe," I said. "You want me to believe that the first time in your life that you ever stole money, you stole a thousand dollars? That's not how people steal. They steal one dollar. Then they steal five dollars. Then ten. Then 50. Then 100. Then 500. *Then* they steal 1000. That's how they steal."

"Honest," she pleaded, "this is my first time."

"Then let me ask you this. Why did you steal a thousand dollars in cash? What did you need the money for?"

This woman looked at her pastor, then at me, and with a straight face said, "I needed the money to cover bad checks."

Do you see how this woman had rationalized her sin? She thought she hadn't stolen anything until she stole a thousand dollars from my ministry. "Don't you realize that you stole this money before you took it from me?" I asked her. "Don't you realize that every time you gave a merchant a check for merchandise without having funds to cover that check, you were stealing merchandise from that store?"

Later, in further counseling with her pastor, she confessed that she had actually stolen 2500 dollars from the ministry. And the pattern was just as I described. First she had taken five dollars for lunch. Next it was 20 dollars to buy a sweater. And so it grew. With crusade offerings there's a lot of cash, and I wouldn't miss a few dollars. Even when she stole 100 dollars and then 200, I didn't miss it. But when she took a thousand, I knew something was wrong.

That's how sin is: It starts small and builds until it becomes a habit. And habits are hard to break. The more you indulge them, the more they occupy your thoughts and your time. If it takes time to build that habit, it usually takes time to reverse it. I've heard testimonies of people who say that God completely and instantly freed them from the pull of drugs or alcohol or sex or whatever their problem was. I know those testimonies are real; God can instantly change a person. But the majority of adult Christians I know have a different experience. They find that just as it took time to develop their bad habits, so it takes time to reverse them. God's power is just as real, but it takes time to see the results. God has to change those powerful drives and rechannel them.

Before I stopped drinking alcohol, I used to spend four or five hours a night drinking. When I quit, I didn't know what to do with all the extra time and the extra money. I was no longer spending 100 or 150 dollars a week on alcohol and cigarettes. My income hadn't changed—just my lifestyle.

In AA they tell the guy who's just stopped drinking, "Thirty meetings in 30 days." Why? Because he's got to do something during the time that he previously spent getting drunk. Suppose the guy meets Christ and goes to church instead; how many hours will his church activities occupy? Five hours a week? That's not enough. It probably took him five hours a *day* to get drunk. During the first year I was sober I built a lot of furniture. I had to *do* something to fill the time I used to spend drinking.

I've run into a few churches that provide a coffee shop that they operate at a loss. They usually don't serve food—just self-serve coffee or soda pop. This provides a place for people to go and talk. Suppose someone has frequented meat markets three nights a week for several years. Now at eight on Friday night, when she used to be preparing to go out and find a partner for sex, she has nothing to do. She needs someplace to go. Or suppose someone has an urge to drink at 6:00 P.M. With the church-sponsored coffee shop he can go and talk with other people until he's too tired to do anything else or the last bar shuts down.

Of course, over the weeks and months a person begins to fill his time with other new activities. He begins to get involved in church-related activities. He develops new relationships. He redirects his attention to family and friends. While I was touring the country promoting my first book, I spent three days in Boston. I was provided with a chauffeur, a young Italian man, to take me to all my appearances. Shortly after he picked me up at the airport he identified himself as a Christian and said, "I was saved out of heroin." The second night there, he invited me to his home for dinner and I met his wife and baby. In his home I noticed a large picture of a boat that intrigued me. When I remarked what great work the model ship was, he showed me some more photographs. "I built it. If you'd like, I'll show it to you tomorrow."

The next day during a break in our schedule, he showed me the model ship, which was on display at a downtown store. It was an exact replica of an old sailing ship. He had built it from a kit that cost nearly 300 dollars. Every single board was real wood and had to be fitted into place individually. Every string and every sail was individually attached. The ship took hundreds of hours to assemble. I had seen such boats in specialty shops and knew they cost as much as 3000 dollars to buy fully assembled. He told me it took him more than 700 hours to build, and he completed it in less than a year. I doubt that many of us could find that much time in our busy schedules.

"I had to do something after I got off heroin," he explained. "I used to spend the night crawling through windows, stealing in order to get money for my drug. It took me six, seven hours a day to get a fix. Now all that was gone." He also had a lot more money, because his income was no longer going to support his habit. He told me with pride that he now owned his limo outright.

I know men in AA who have amazing hobbies—model building, fishing, flying airplanes. They're very good at these activities because they have patience that most of us don't have. Instead of hurrying through something, they want to fill their time. So rather than hammering together a piece of furniture in half an hour, they'll take four hours and do it right. After a year they begin to man the telephones and counsel other alcoholics. That's a great way to fill time—by helping others.

There is evidence that the sexual revolution that has so consumed our society may be winding down. For the most part it has little to do with a changing moral climate. Recently a survey on political issues in the South revealed that the number two concern of Americans (behind employment) was AIDS. They have legitimate reason to be concerned. Twenty-five million Europeans died during the Black Plague in the mid-1300's. In the eighteenth century as many as 400,000 people died of smallpox. A flu epidemic in 1917-18 killed 500,000 Americans. Polio infected some 400,000 Americans between 1943 and 1956. Horrible as those plagues were, the AIDS epidemic threatens to overshadow them all.

Already we see the devastation in certain countries of central Africa. Between two and five million Africans are now carriers of the virus, and at least 50,000 have already died. Countries like Uganda and Zambia must face the fact that the disease is affecting as much as 30 percent of their young adults.

By 1991 AIDS will have claimed more American lives than the wars in Vietnam and Korea combined.[3] When I mention some of these facts in churches, I can tell by the expressions in the congregation that some of the people sitting in those pews think they may be carriers. And they're rightly terrified of that prospect. More and more people will be affected in coming years.

I believe that the AIDS epidemic presents the church with an incredible opportunity—if we don't blow it. People are realizing that the price of sin is steep. The church has an opportunity to give hope to AIDS victims, if we don't drive them away out of fear. Some church leaders have publicly proclaimed AIDS as God's judgment against the homosexual and drug community. It may be, but we need to be careful not to condemn people so severely that they aren't free to come to our churches for help. We must also realize that increasingly AIDS is being transmitted through heterosexual contact. It's true that many people have and will pay a steep price for their promiscuity, but it's also true that God offers forgiveness to all who are willing to come. He turns none away, and neither can we.

Some people are promoting condoms as the way to stop the spread of AIDS. That's a mistake. Condoms can't even stop pregnancy. Women get pregnant every year by men who wear condoms. Condoms are only 80 percent effective. The publicity is providing a false hope to keep the "sexual revolution" alive.

AIDS is spread by the sharing of body fluids. That includes deep sexual kissing, which our schools tell our kids is just fine. Planned Parenthood views pregnancy as the greatest potential evil to teens. "Stop pregnancy, not sex" is their battle cry. But promiscuity is the real problem, and soon the church will be filling up with its victims.

We must separate the sin from the sinner. And we must separate fact from fiction concerning AIDS. No one can be infected just by sitting next to someone who is infected by the AIDS virus. In the coming years, numerous victims and their families will need care. The church can help provide that care.

At the same time, the sin of promiscuity must be addressed. The church needs to be in the forefront of promoting the only sure vaccine against AIDS and other venereal diseases—abstinence and monogamy.

1. Kathie Durbin, "Young Voices: A Youth Forum," in *The Oregonian*, Mar. 22, 1987, Arts and Entertainment section, p. 6.
2. Gregory Fossedal, "Dartmouth's X-Rated Student Literature," in *Human Events*, Mar. 7, 1987.
3. "Aids: At the Dawn of Fear," in *U.S. News and World Report*, Jan. 12, 1987, p. 60.

8

IN PURSUIT OF HAPPINESS

In my hometown, a suburban community about 25 miles from downtown Dallas, there's a huge grocery/department store that is open 24 hours a day. I stopped there one night at 1:00 A.M. on my way home from the airport (having just returned from a speaking tour) to pick up some milk and a couple of other food items.

While I was walking down one aisle, I noticed a woman standing with her empty cart in the middle of the aisle, apparently trying to decide what to buy. I thought little of it and continued with my shopping. A few moments later I returned down that aisle toward the checkout stand and noticed that the woman hadn't moved. In fact, she was crying. So I stopped and said, "Pardon me, ma'am. Can I help you find something?"

At that she started to bawl as she said, "I can't find anything I want."

I quickly noted that this woman was very well dressed. And in this store she could buy just about anything she might possibly want—from appliances to clothes to exotic gourmet foods. Apparently she had the means to purchase anything in the store, and maybe that was her problem. A few aisles over was a coffee shop, so I suggested, "Let's go over and sit down and have a cup of coffee."

As we sat down the woman mumbled, "I've been here since midnight. I've been wandering all over this store, but I can't find anything I want. I know I need something. Something's missing, but I don't know what it is."

I asked her a few questions and confirmed that this woman and her husband were very successful financially. She admitted that for years, whenever she had a need, she was able to buy something to meet that need. "Maybe what you're missing isn't something you can buy here," I suggested. She looked up at me, slightly perplexed. "In fact, it's something you can't buy anywhere."

"What are you talking about?"

"Maybe what you need is something that will truly fulfill you, and it has nothing to do with the material things of life. Just out of curiosity, do you go to church?"

The woman, her hands wrapped around her coffee cup, answered, "No. I haven't gone to church since I was a teenager."

"Well, is it possible that the thing that's missing in your life is spiritual? Maybe it's something you can't buy for any price. But it's available for free."

With that I began to tell this woman about Jesus Christ. I briefly reviewed my own background. "For 33 years I tried to get fulfillment from things like alcohol, sex, cigarettes, and money, but I always had an emptiness in my life. That emptiness was filled by a relationship with Jesus Christ."

She shook her head and said sadly, "I couldn't do that. My husband and I have too much. We're too rich to get involved with religion."

"Since when did Christ say you had to be poor to be a Christian?" I countered. "Christ didn't say you have to give everything to the church in order to have His grace." Then I explained to her how she could enter into a relationship with Christ and led her in a prayer as she opened the door of her life to Jesus Christ. The following Sunday, she and her husband started attending church.

In contrast to some of the other kinds of Transition Christians we've mentioned in the book, this couple had no trouble assimilating into the church. They were not involved in any perversions. They did not have problems with alcohol or drugs. They were welcomed into the church with open arms. But few if any people in the congregation realized their deep spiritual needs.

I don't know if this couple would qualify as "Yuppies," that group of baby-boomers that now control almost one quarter of the national income.[1] For these people, life's top priority is the acquisition of material wealth. Their status is defined by what they own. The solution to every problem is to go out and buy something to fix it. Often their biggest problems are with their children, which aren't so easy to fix. If a son is having problems at school, Dad buys him something to make him feel better. If a daughter is seeing a certain boy too much, the parents send her to Europe (where she winds up having a series of one-night stands).

Many Yuppies were actually brought up in Christian homes and they went to church as kids. But that doesn't mean they developed spiritually. They often rejected the value system of Christianity. I was disheartened to learn that one of the men who pushed for the launch of the space shuttle Challenger that exploded, killing seven astronauts, was a deacon in a Baptist church. He had a schedule to meet and he was going to get that ship off the pad no matter what. He was willing to take chances he should not have taken, and now he is retired as a result of what happened.

This is only one example of the attitude of the Yuppie generation that's invading our churches. Too many Christians want to emulate the success of this group. They think they have arrived when they have that nice house in the most exclusive neighborhood, with a BMW in the driveway. They want their pastor to look successful too, so they buy him a Cadillac or Lincoln. But the increasing numbers of Yuppies who are pouring into our churches are coming because that lifestyle isn't the source of a fulfilling life.

My Uncle Irv is certainly no Yuppie, but in him I see the emptiness of materialism. Recently he called me up and said he had just bought a new telephone. "Irv, I just bought you a new phone four months ago!" I replied.

"I know, but I didn't like it, so I bought another one."

"What did you do with the old one?"

"Oh, I just tossed it."

"You threw away a 150-dollar phone! Irv, why didn't you at least sell it? Surely you could have gotten 20 or 30 bucks for it at a pawnshop!"

"I don't know," he said meekly. And that's just the point. He *doesn't* know why he throws out his perfectly good raincoat and buys another, why he's constantly moving the furniture around in his apartment, why he's always replacing the pictures on his wall. He's never satisfied, and he will never be satisfied until he discovers that what he's missing is found only in Jesus Christ.

It's so easy to look at the nice homes which the Yuppies have and think that this is what we want. But we don't see the pain behind those nice walls. We don't see the price they've paid for that success—the emptiness, the rebellion of their children, the loneliness. Family happiness is surrendered in order to have all those material things. When the Yuppie finally shows up in church, the lifelong Christian has no idea what he went through to get there. He might have it all materially, but he's probably miserable spiritually.

Mike and Lorna are a good example of two people who were accepted too fast into the heart of the church because of their public success. Lorna had started a small windowshade business out of their home ten years earlier. It grew so rapidly that Mike quit his job and joined her. Soon Mike had taken over the business and Lorna had returned to being a housewife.

With nothing to do and more than a little resentment at having Mike take over her business, she became involved in community affairs. That led her into a close relationship with a pastor's wife. Not long after this Lorna accepted Christ and talked her husband into accompanying her to church, where he also met the Lord.

Mike and Lorna became close friends of the pastor and his wife—too close, as far as much of the church congregation was concerned. Many old-timers believed that the pastor was playing favorites based on economics. Though the reason for their relationship was not financial, many in the congregation assumed that it was. When the pastor pressed the church board for a raise, many saw his request as an effort to move up to the lifestyle of his new friends. The resulting dispute produced a split in the church.

Pastors need to beware of their relationships with new members who are prosperous—or, for that matter, old members who are prosperous. When a car dealer gives a new car to a pastor every year, the pastor faces a dilemma. If he doesn't tell the church body how he manages to get a new car every year, they will wonder where he gets the money. (Most pastors can't afford a *used* car on what their churches pay, much less a new one.) If he does tell the church, many members will resent the car dealer, who is not able to give everyone in the church the same deal.

For Mike and Lorna, the situation was even more tragic than for the pastor and his split church. Because of their close relationship with the pastor's family, they didn't get the spiritual guidance they needed. The pastor became too close to them to correct some of their spiritual and moral errors. Lorna had really joined the church in order to have something which Mike could not take away from her, the way he had her windowshade business. So when Mike became the center of attention in the church as the pastor's best friend, Lorna began to drink. She was determined that Mike would not deprive her of this area. Eventually that drinking problem ended their marriage.

None of the church members who so envied this couple and their relationship with the pastor could see the tremendous problems in this couple's marriage. All they could see was their BMW parked next to the pastor's car at the better restaurants. If they could have known what was really happening, I doubt that there would have been any envy at all.

The prosperous members of the baby-boom generation who are entering our churches have discovered that no amount of money will fill the void in their lives. Yet the church often fosters this very materialistic attitude. In my church and several others in my town, half the cars are Cadillacs—including mine (honestly, I got a great deal!)—and the other half are Mercedes and BMW's. Okay, so that's an exaggeration, but it sure appears that way. And the message this sends is that only "successful" people need attend this church.

Material wealth is the downfall of many good ministries. Evangelists are definitely not exempt from this temptation. I fly first-class a lot, even though I don't pay for it. I have traveled so many miles for so long in the cheapest section of the plane that the airline I use most frequently elevated me to a special group of frequent flyers. As one of the benefits for flying more than 80,000 miles per year on that one airline, they upgrade me to first class at no extra charge on just about every trip I take. Of course I have to wait on standby for this privilege, and I never know if I am going to get it. But it is a nice perk on those three- and four-hour flights across country.

Has flying first-class spoiled me? To be honest, yes. I like the extra room to work. In fact, a whole lot of the work on this book was done in the first-class section of an airplane. I just don't have the room in a coach seat to spread out the papers and do the job right. But I have to be careful; if I start liking it too much, I will begin to purchase first-class seats when I can't get them free. Unlike my brother's atheist organization, my ministry cannot afford to buy first-class tickets. And no church inviting me across the country is going to reimburse me for first-class seats.

Many times the best meal I get all week is with a pastor's family on Sunday. Most days I eat a hamburger in my car on the way to another meeting or while running an errand. I could get real used to those fancy buffet meals they serve in fine hotels after church. Again, I have to be careful.

It's easy to get accustomed to convenience and nice things. Sometimes wealthy new members of a church or ministry can change the lifestyle of the entire church for the worse without realizing what they are doing. It can really affect people negatively. Many times these new members are only trying to impress people in order to make new friends in the wonderful place they have just found.

A new member at my church who was obviously a Yuppie had a phone in his Mercedes. He and I were talking and he offered to show it to me. It was one of the new cellular models that can be used just like a regular phone, with no operator needed. I was so impressed by the increased productive time he had (being able to conduct business on his way to appointments) that I installed a phone in my own car for a mere 35 dollars a month. There was only one problem: The air time costs an additional 30 cents a minute. That means about a dollar for a three-minute local call.

I spend perhaps three hours a day in my car, and I found that my productivity did increase significantly. I was able to get hold of people without waiting around my office. That was the great part. The bad news was that my phone bill quickly approached 250 dollars per month in air time alone. While I was getting much more accomplished with the car phone, my ministry cannot afford that much in extra communication costs the way the man who introduced the phone to me could.

The church is a place which brings many people from varied backgrounds and economic statuses together under one roof. Each of us must guard against the "keep-up-with-the-Joneses" nature of mankind. And it is not just a matter of worry to ministers and evangelists.

I know a man—I'll call him Burt—who ran his very successful business into bankruptcy by purchasing a business jet and a jet helicopter. He did not need them for his type of business, but they were prestige items. Why did he buy them? Burt's best friend in the church sold them to him "cheap" because his company was buying an even bigger jet and an even faster helicopter. Burt found out, too late, that he could not afford to imitate the lifestyle of church members whom God had blessed with better circumstances.

Let's face it—when we're talking about the values of our nation, we are an atheistic country. Too many Christians are not taking their faith out of the pew and putting it into practice in their daily lives. We conduct our day-to-day exchanges in a totally materialistic, atheistic manner, with no concern for the spiritual nature of what we're doing. Many Christian businessmen do not follow biblical guidelines in their business. For example, it's wrong to give a man a job unless you can pay that man enough to take care of his family.

Listen to what the apostle James says: "Behold, the pay of the laborers who mowed your fields, and which has been withheld by you, cries out against you. . . . You have lived luxuriously on the earth and led a life of wanton pleasure" (James 5:4,5).

If you're a Christian businessman, and a man with a wife and four kids comes to you and applies for a $4.75-an-hour job, you don't give that man the job unless you are willing to pay him more. It's obvious that this man cannot afford to support his family on $4.75 an hour. But we do not have very many businessmen in this country who take into consideration what an individual needs to survive. In fact many "Christian" businessmen pride themselves on making the most amount of money for the least amount of labor cost. In the past such attitudes have led to the formation of vicious labor unions that don't care about slashing people's tires or threatening a man's family members—because that's how they feel they were treated. Many employers have gotten back exactly what they dished out to their employees.

I see another sign of this materialistic mind-set at most churches where I speak. Usually after a service where I've preached, I'm invited to lunch or dinner with the pastor and a handful of influential people in that congregation. Who are these people who have the "privilege" of dining with the guest speaker? The owner of the largest local business. The vice-president of the local bank. The contractor who built the church parking lot at no cost to the church. The couple that's given the most financially to the congregation. They sit around the table in sort of an unspoken pecking order.

In this church are there any reformed alcoholics or drug-users or sexual perverts? Probably. But they are rarely invited to this meal. They come and hear me speak in church, but it is those who are materially endowed who get invited to dinner. That doesn't help me remember my past, and it probably doesn't help the pastor keep a healthy perspective of his congregation.

Now I will say that those meals aren't a total waste. For my benefit as well as theirs I inevitably challenge these men and women with some of the tough issues we've tried to address in this book. But why is it that those who are closest to the preacher usually are the most materially successful? In too many congregations, a person's financial statement is also used to determine his spiritual condition.

John was a man who did very well in the oil industry for many years. He helped support my ministry, and gave large amounts of money to his church during the five years after he accepted Christ. His church was one of the many "name-it-and-claim-it" congregations in Dallas. Then the oil business had a dramatic downturn, and John ran into financial problems and finally lost his business. He wound up selling his home to pay off some of his debts, and then he, his wife, and their three children wound up living in a sleazy motel room just a few blocks from their church.

Naturally John turned to his church for help. Several elders came over to "counsel" him. These men explained that the reason John had lost his business was because he had moved away from God and did not have the proper spiritual life. Therefore, the church could not help him because he was not "living for Christ."

I want to be very careful here, because I realize that most churches don't have such a callous attitude. But many Christians do believe that the condition of your bank account is directly proportionate to your spiritual walk with Christ. I have problems with that. I seriously doubt that the entire oil industry collapsed simply for the purpose of knocking John out of business because he wasn't living a spiritual life. Maybe God was trying to teach all oilmen, or the United States, a lesson. But I doubt that it all had to do with that one man.

The problem which James so sternly addressed in his epistle is still a part of the church. He specifically condemned the attitude of favoritism: "If a man comes into your assembly with a gold ring and dressed in fine clothes, and there also comes in a poor man in dirty clothes, and you pay special attention to the one who is wearing the fine clothes . . . have you not made distinctions among yourselves, and become judges with evil motives?" (James 2:2-4).

It's amazing how many Christians want to point out the promises of Scripture that promote wealth and happiness for us on this earth. But they conveniently ignore such words as these, again from James: "Come now, you rich, weep and howl for your miseries which are coming upon you. Your riches have rotted and your garments have become moth-eaten" (James 5:1,2). That's a promise too. To me this is simply a reminder that all material possessions and wealth are temporary. They will soon pass away. They aren't all that important compared to the issues of the kingdom of heaven.

Perhaps the most dramatic illustration I've seen of this principle was in a Florida coastal community. A woman who had accepted Christ as her Lord and Savior managed to convince her husband to come and hear me speak at a crusade. He was an atheist, but he came because he was also a staunch anticommunist, and my anticommunist reputation had preceded my evangelistic reputation in that area of the country.

That night this man identified so much with my message that he came forward during my invitation and surrendered his life to Christ. The couple returned again the next night and again came forward during the invitation. "We need some help," the woman said to me. "We have discussed this and we don't know what to do. You see, we don't own a home. We live on a yacht . . ."

Her husband interrupted. "Could you come with us back to our boat? It would be easier to talk about it there."

After the service I rode with them to the marina and boarded their yacht. It was as fine a boat as I've ever been on, and I was impressed. "I can see why you live on this," I said. "Do you travel quite a bit?"

"We go down to the islands quite regularly," the man said. Then he motioned to me and I followed him below deck. He put his hand on one of the panels and pulled, and a secret compartment opened up. In it were several large rolls of burlap. He unrolled one of them to expose numerous plastic bags of drugs. There were several thousand dollars worth just in that single roll of burlap.

He turned to me and and said, "This boat cost us nearly a million dollars. It costs thousands to maintain it. Neither my wife nor I can make that kind of money doing anything else. If we stop running drugs, we'll have to give up this boat and everything else we have. We have no idea where we'll go or what we'll do."

I sat down, trying to comprehend what this couple was telling me. I sensed that they had gotten very comfortable with their lifestyle. Now that they were Christians, they were reluctant to give it up. Yet I had to tell them the truth. "You cannot live for Christ and Satan," I said. "You cannot be Satan's tool and sell chemicals to children that you know will kill them."

"Neither of us use drugs," the woman interjected. "And we can give a lot to the church."

"Yes, but you're providing drugs for those kids and it can destroy them. And it will destroy you spiritually as well. How can you go to church and tithe off your proceeds while you know you're killing children? God doesn't want your money. He doesn't need your tithe off this kind of activity. You'll please Him much more if you get out of this business and trust Him to direct you into a new line of work."

"You're right," the man sighed. He was silent for a moment, then he said, "Let's take a ride." We motored out of the harbor into the open sea. A mile from shore I helped this couple haul the drugs up onto the deck and toss them overboard. That night perhaps a million dollars worth of drugs sank into the ocean, along with several automatic weapons.

Wealth alone has never made anything right. Prosperity was not something we could measure a successful man or church by in biblical times, and it still is not today.

Seeking material wealth can be as habit-forming as sex or drugs. Just ask the "inside traders" of Wall Street. After the first ten million dollars, what makes them cheat for a hundred million more? Certainly it is not the call of Christ.

I'm also amazed at the lack of financial commitment to God's work among some Christians. Once I led a Communist to Christ, and when he found out he was expected to give 10 percent of his income to the church he was flabbergasted. He had given between 30 and 50 percent of his income to the Communist party for years! My mother's atheist organization doesn't have a large number of members, but she has received millions and millions of dollars, far more than any church with an equivalent number of members. The reason is simple: Atheists have a lot more at stake in proving they are right. If I as a Christian am wrong about the existence of God, I won't suffer as a result. But atheists feel compelled to pay whatever price is necessary to prove that there is no God, because if there is one, they're in big trouble. Too many Christians would rather hold onto their "hard-earned" money than invest it in God's work.

There is another call that came to me as a Transition Christian. It's a call that many Christians have heard for 2000 years—the call to stop living for material gain and to follow Christ's example in ministry. Unlike some, I didn't go into the ministry willingly. I was doing just fine without that responsibility. Yet today I would never go back to the rat race of trying to acquire wealth. It is the one thing I can do to hopefully minimize the damage my mother has done through her "ministry."

1. Charles W. Colson, "A Call to Rescue the Yuppies," in *Christianity Today*, May 17, 1985, p. 17.

9

HOGTIED INTO THE MINISTRY

What exactly does my mother do? Most people recognize her as a highly visible spokeswoman for the atheist viewpoint in America. Her organization, American Atheists, is "dedicated to the complete and absolute separation of state and church." Among their stated objectives are "to stimulate and promote freedom of thought and inquiry concerning religious beliefs" and "the establishment and maintenance of a thoroughly secular system of education" as well as the development and propagation of "a social philosophy in which man is the central figure, who alone must be the source of strength, progress, and ideals for the well-being and happiness of all humanity."

These goals are carried out primarily through her national conventions and the publication of materials, particularly the monthly magazine *American Atheist*. A brief look at one issue will give you an idea of their methods. The December 1986 issue features a crucifixion scene on the cover. Santa Claus is nailed to the center cross and two elves hang on crosses on either side. Santa's sack, full of presents, is lying at the base of the cross, and boys and girls, all with frowns on their faces, are pulling packages out of the sack.

American Atheists don't believe in Christmas—actually they resent it—and instead prefer to celebrate the winter solstice. My mother writes that Christians "stole . . . one of the most beautiful holidays in the world" in her article "The Solstice Season." My brother then writes about the ongoing battle of American atheists to remove manger scenes from all public schools and county courthouses. He talks about various legal actions, past and present, and why the atheists must not rest until all religious symbols are banned from public property.

There's a short story in this issue called "Satan Claus." It's about a Christian woman who teaches her daughter that Santa Claus is evil, actually a cover for Satan, and that anyone who believes in Santa is going to hell. The daughter tells the neighbor boy, who thinks that's the craziest idea ever. The boy's father decides to dress up as Santa and pay a visit to his neighbor in order to show her that Santa is not such a bad guy. The Christian woman promptly freaks out and shoots him in the foot.

Finally, there are several pages of information debunking every aspect of the biblical account of Christ's birth. With a mixture of misinformation and sarcasm the writer "proves" that Jesus wasn't born of a virgin, laughs at the allegedly contradictory genealogies in Matthew and Luke, disputes the Old Testament prophecies that support Jesus' claim as Messiah, and mocks the story of the star that appeared at Jesus' birth.

That's the kind of inflammatory material that comes out of my mother's "ministry." My brother, Jon Garth, and my daughter Robin are part of her ministry team. And to think that I helped create that monster during the two years I worked with my mother in Austin, Texas! There's no way I can undo the damage caused by that work, but my desire is to exercise some damage control, to try to slow down the influence of that group.

It was never my intention to start a ministry after I met Jesus Christ. But my letters to the Baltimore and Austin newspapers generated a lot of publicity and pushed me into the limelight. Four months after my conversion I was flown to Washington D.C. to appear with Jerry Falwell and Jesse Helms at a pro-school prayer rally. They didn't want me to say anything; I felt I was there just to be shown off like some kind of prize turkey. Perhaps they expected a burned-out old drunk. I think I surprised everyone present, including the news media, when I pleaded my case to allow God to have equal time with atheism in schools.

Shortly after that, an itinerant preacher by the name of Wayne Neal visited me in Houston. This dear man travels a continuous loop around the country visiting churches and preaching. I remember him visiting my mother at our home in Baltimore and again in Austin, trying to convert her to Christ. "Have you been invited to speak at any churches?" he asked me.

"What do you mean?" I asked. I didn't know people got invited to speak at churches. At the little church I was attending, we didn't have guest speakers.

"You need to tell your story in churches," he answered. He picked up the phone and called the pastor of the Central Assembly of God Church in Austin and arranged for me to speak there in early June.

"But what am I going to tell them?" I protested.

"Just tell them your story."

To be honest, I had no idea what he meant. I didn't think I had a story to tell. Actually I was a decent public speaker, since I had given lots of lectures to young airline managers and supervisors. But I wasn't prepared to speak about Christianity. The only thing I could figure out was that they probably wanted to know what atheism was like.

So I jotted down a few notes and went to speak about how miserable it was being raised in an atheistic home. After 15 minutes I ran out of things to say and the pastor tried to fill the rest of the time with a question-and-answer session.

The itinerant preacher lined up some other engagements for me. So here I was, less than five months old spiritually, talking in churches, still smoking three packs of cigarettes a day, still not sure what had happened in my life when I "got saved," and trying to figure out what I was supposed to say when I stood behind a pulpit. After each speaking engagement I would meet people in the church foyer and try to field questions like "Did your family really know Lee Harvey Oswald?" and "How come your mother became an atheist?" But mostly they wanted to know what convinced me to leave atheism and embrace Christ.

I knew that something was wrong with my speech. Obviously I wasn't telling people what they wanted to hear or else they wouldn't be asking so many questions. I thought they wanted to learn what atheism and humanism were all about. So I told them all about my life before Christ. But they wanted to hear a testimony. At the time I didn't even know what that was, but I could tell by the questions that it had something to do with how my life was changing.

Finally I took a legal pad of paper and started writing down all the questions I was being asked. I wound up with nearly a hundred questions. I wrote them in chronological order on four-by-six file cards and then answered each question. The next time I was invited to speak, early in 1981, I took those cards and made that my talk. Without stating the questions, I blended the information together and wound up with a 45-minute message that seemed to grip the audience.

Soon after that I ran up against another problem. I was speaking one Sunday morning at two church services. After the first service the pastor asked me, "Bill, why don't you give the invitation?" As usual, I had given my talk, then sat down while the pastor invited those who wanted to accept Christ or rededicate their lives to come forward. Three people came forward, but this pastor said, "Your message was so powerful that it breaks the flow if I get up to give the invitation. I believe we would have had three times more people saved this morning if you had done the invitation."

What was I to do? I didn't know how to give an invitation. With panic, I flipped through my Bible and tried to find some verses I could use. After my message in the second service, I stumbled through what must rank as the worst invitation any evangelist has ever given. And then I looked in shock as 18 people came forward, including two deacons. In a powerful way, God showed me that He was using me. But I certainly didn't understand how or why.

Soon after that I was approached by Thomas Nelson Publishers and asked to write a book. I can say now that I shouldn't have written *My Life Without God* at that point. It was too early. It proved to be one of the most difficult experiences of my life. I started with a ghostwriter but ended up writing the book myself in hotel rooms and on airplanes while flying from coast to coast to give my testimony.

However, the book did provide one great benefit, for writing about my experiences was like a gigantic psychotherapy session. It forced me to examine my life chronologically and to see the mistakes I had made. It helped me switch hostility away from my mother. People find it hard to believe that I never really hated my mother. Sure, I despised what she did, but writing the book helped me admit that I was a sinner too. There were a lot of sordid things about my past that up until then I had not been willing to face. My writing became an honest confession of my sins before God which allowed me to bring closure to my life before Christ.

Despite the benefit, the process was painful. In order to meet the publisher's deadline, I finished the manuscript in Las Vegas, figuring that no one would look for me there. Reviewing my life on paper was so depressing that one afternoon I went down to the hotel kitchen, got 100 nonreturnable pop bottles, and put them in the trunk of my car. Then I bought 200 rounds of ammunition for my .38 special and headed into the desert. I took out my hostility by breaking all 100 pop bottles with just 106 rounds!

Finally the book was written, but unfortunately the worst was yet to come. Though I had confessed my sins before God and He had promised that "as far as the east is from the west, so far has He removed our transgressions from us" (Psalm 103:12), the public wasn't about to forget. They were encouraged to read all about it. In order to promote sales of the book in secular stores, the publisher hired as publicist a woman who was a mirror image of my mother. She had no concept of Christianity, but she knew how to garner media attention, and she organized my publicity tour.

In Detroit, one talkshow hostess was literally in tears as she asked me, "Why do you hate your mother?" Of course, she hadn't read the book; she had only looked over the promotional material. I did *not* hate my mother, and that was not the subject of my book. In fact, *My Life Without God* was an uncomplimentary autobiography. I could have come out a lot better by not being so truthful, and no one would have known the difference. This was a book where the title very accurately described the contents; it was a revelation of how sin destroys a life and a family.

Of course, it was almost impossible to correct the wrong perceptions that interviewers had. The publicist was trying to create a controversy at the level of *Mommy Dearest*, and while she may have succeeded, it was destroying me. Finally I had to end the tour prematurely. I simply could not continue reliving the hell of my past.

The formation of my ministry actually grew out of an attempt to reopen contact with my family. Since my conversion I had not been able to communicate with my mother, brother, or daughter, either by phone or by mail. Every time I had tried to call my mother she had hung up on me. A Mother's Day card for my mother and birthday cards to my brother and daughter Robin were torn up and mailed back. I could not make any contacts.

So in April of 1981 I decided to go to Salt Lake City, where my mother was holding her annual American Atheists convention. These conventions are really evangelistic crusades, for they are one of the primary ways that my mother recruits new members. She goes into a city, generates as much publicity as possible so people come to her meetings, then attempts to win them to the cause.

To try to counteract her influence, I purchased a half-page ad in the daily newspaper to tell the delegates that Jesus Christ loved them. There was a phone number for anyone who wanted to call for more information. A small Assembly of God church agreed to man the phones and counsel those who called.

Because of the publicity my mother generated, plus my ad, the newspaper interviewed me. I was shocked and surprised to see the next day that the front page of one section was divided in half, with a bold black line down the middle. On one side was the story about my mother and her convention. On the other side was the story of my conversion. They had given me exactly one-half of the coverage even though I had no organization and even though my crusade, if you could even call it that, wouldn't draw one-tenth of the crowds that the American Atheists did.

That week I didn't achieve my first goal of making contact with my family. But a lot of people did call in response to the ad. A few were vicious, but most were from Christians who appreciated the efforts being made to counter the damage the atheists were doing. And the publicity showed me something very significant: No matter where I went or how large or small my program was, if there was an atheist convention the news media would give me 50 percent of the coverage just because of my background.

After that experience in Salt Lake City I decided to form an organization that would organize crusades and outreach events in conjunction with atheist conventions around the country. And not just my mother's, either. Some people think I only follow my mother around the country and bother her. This ministry goes to all atheist conventions, such as the Freedom from Religion Foundation, American Humanist Association, American Rationalist Association, National Association for the Advancement of Atheism, and American Secularization. We have people go in and monitor the conventions so we know exactly what they're promoting. And we're ready to talk to delegates and their family members as they come and go from the hotel.

The ministry idea was logical, considering my background, but I had no experience and little counsel to help me get off the ground. For example, I made a major mistake in my choice of a name. I was reading the words of the apostle Paul, "No man can lay a foundation other than the one which is laid, which is Jesus Christ" (1 Corinthians 3:11). Since the foundation of my faith was Jesus Christ, it seemed logical to call my ministry "William J. Murray Faith Foundation, Inc." It never even dawned on me that someone might think that I had formed a foundation to give away money. But that's what people thought. They figured I was ashamed of my past and so I was giving away money to make up for my sins. That certainly wasn't the case; what personal assets I had were mostly put into the ministry to help get it off the ground. But that perception made it almost impossible to raise money. I was quickly forced to change the name to "Murray Faith Ministries."

I was also concerned that my name was part of the organization name. I didn't want my name on it; I wanted this to be for the glory of God. But I was advised that people would not support the work unless there was a highly visible name attached to it.

One reason I had to pour my own assets into the ministry was that I didn't have any family to assist me. Someone from a Christian family who wants to go into the ministry usually has encouragement and practical help. Sister comes over and types. Brother volunteers to set up the sound equipment. Wife answers the phones and plays the piano or sings at the meetings. Father and Grandfather throw some seed money into the pot to help the young minister get started.

I had no such family support. My brother was helping my mother's organization get bigger and bigger. My daughter was editing her magazine. Me—I was the black sheep of the family. I was the one who had turned against the family and forsaken my atheistic, left-wing beliefs. Also, my wife had filed for divorce and run off with an atheist.

Where could I turn for help? The only place I knew was the church. Unfortunately, because of the book and my ministry at Salt Lake City, I was now being invited to speak all over the country. I was probably in my home church only once a month. So I really didn't know very many people.

One day I felt a desperate need for help in getting a mailing out. I called the church and asked the secretary if she knew where I could get some help. "I'd be glad to make some calls for you," she said cheerfully. "How much should I tell them you're paying?"

This is not a negative reflection on my church or the secretary. But it sure would have been different if I had grown up in that church. If I had been in that congregation for 20 or 30 years and then went into the ministry, I would have had plenty of friends. There would have been many people I could have called who would have gladly volunteered to help some afternoon or evening, stuffing envelopes or typing labels.

Some people think that I'm in the ministry because of the money. I have to laugh, because this is a losing proposition financially. I'd be much better off sitting behind an oak desk somewhere. But when God calls you, what can you do? Actually, God didn't call me to the ministry. He hogtied me and threw me in! This wasn't my idea; I'd much rather be doing something else. But circumstances made it obvious that this was God's will. And I think He's kept me in the ministry by keeping me poor. The ministry has never had any extra funds. There are times when I've wanted to walk away from it but couldn't because I would leave debts. I couldn't walk away from those obligations without harming the cause of Christ.

Besides, there are so many people who have come to a real relationship with Christ at my meetings. More than 7000 in 1986 alone, and perhaps 50,000 during my years of ministry, have trusted Christ. How could I let those people down and give up the ministry? Sure, the ministry is a struggle; it's a 24-hour-a-day job. It's more than just preaching; it's carrying boxes of books and tracts in and out of meetings, plus endless hours of answering the same questions over and over again. But it is also watching God perform modern-day miracles in the form of changed lives.

Probably most difficult for me is the way the past jumps up to grab me at the most inopportune times. My reputation refuses to die. Some people will never believe that my conversion is genuine. Others are confused by the actions of my younger brother. Not long ago it was reported that Jon Murray, the son of Madalyn Murray O'Hair, spent a couple of nights at the home of Larry Flynt, publisher of *Hustler* magazine. Some people saw this report and thought I was the one who spent the nights in Flynt's home. "Everyone knows what goes on in Larry Flynt's home!" they said as they questioned my walk with Christ. Well, everyone may know what goes on in that home, *but I wasn't there to watch*! It just so happens that Madalyn Murray O'Hair has *two* sons. One is Christian, the other is atheistic. It's amazing how much confusion this results in and how many problems it causes me.

The worst case of mistaken identity occurred in 1985, and I still occasionally feel the impact. The Bob Larson program out of Denver invited Jon to come on the show and talk about what atheists believe. Bob thought it would help the cause of Christ by exposing Jon's beliefs to the Christian community. I knew about the program and was asked to be on the following show to challenge my brother's statements. While I got a few calls about that, it provided little problem for me or my ministry.

However, shortly after this program several other Christian radio and TV stations thought that having a genuine atheist appear on one of their programs was a good idea. One station in Los Angeles put Jon on a morning show during drive time. At the beginning of the program they identified him as Jon Murray, the atheist son of Madalyn Murray O'Hair. But then for the rest of the broadcast they only referred to him as the son of atheist leader Madalyn Murray O'Hair. People in their cars who missed the start of the program were treated to all sorts of blasphemy and incredible statements to the effect that Jesus Christ never existed and that if He did, he was probably a homosexual.

Christians listening to that program were totally confused. They had heard that the son of Madalyn Murray O'Hair had become a Christian and was now an evangelist. Immediately I received phone calls and letters demanding, "Is it true? Have you really gone back to atheism?" Two years later I still received such calls on occasion. "I just heard a rumor that you're no longer a Christian," they inevitably started. Those rumors go back to my brother's exposure on a Christian station.

My problem isn't unique. Transition Christians constantly have to live down their past, whether they go into the ministry or not. Chuck Colson of Watergate fame faced those caustic remarks when his conversion became public. Many people thought the only reason he turned to Christ was because he figured it was the only way he would be able to make money once he got out of prison. Many people feel the same about me; they think I'm only a Christian to make money off my past. I'm sure Chuck Colson would agree with me—if it's money we want, we'd do a lot better in the secular world.

Another problem is that there will always be people who remember me the way I was and refuse to believe I've really changed. Every Transition Christian must face this problem even if he doesn't have family members who embarrass him publicly. If he wants to go into ministry, there will be some people who remember how rotten he was and won't accept him as a minister or an evangelist. One person even said to me, "Bill, you're just an old drunk trying to make a living any way you can."

In addition, it seems that we Transition Christians have to live up to a tougher standard in the ministry. I am not going to lie to you and say I have never gotten angry in the ministry, or that I have never done any wrong as a Christian. Recently I blew up at my office staff after they took a two-hour lunch break and let the answering service handle all the phones. "Just what were you thinking?" I demanded of them. "Why am I paying four people in this office between six and eight dollars an hour if the answering service is going to answer all the phone calls? Apparently I don't need you four people; I only need my answering service."

I'll admit I didn't handle that situation very well. If that was the only glimpse you had had of me as a Christian, you could well get the impression that I'm not very spiritual. You might conclude that I haven't changed much over the years as a Christian. You might even doubt that I'm a Christian. All I can say in my defense are the words of a popular Christian bumper sticker: "Christians aren't perfect, just forgiven."

At this point I have to say that it's not just Transition Christians who struggle with perceptions and who must endure tremendous pressure trying to live perfect lives. When any Christian figure who is in the public eye stumbles, it's a reflection on all of us Christians. I first heard about the scandal of Jim and Tammy Bakker while I was on a speaking tour in Great Britain. It was embarrassing to read in London's *Sunday Times* the headline: "TV Preachers Get Down in the Dirt." I cringed at the sarcastic put-downs; this was a big joke to the non-Christian world.

But I sympathize with this couple that has been in the spotlight. On television the Bakkers had to play the part of the perfectly married couple. It was courageous for Tammy to even admit that she had an addiction problem and was taking treatment at the Betty Ford Center. But when news broke about Jim's affair with a church secretary seven years before, and the financial payoffs to keep her quiet, it put an end to their ministry for the time being as Jerry Falwell took over control of the PTL ministry.

I think probably all of us in ministry have one or two embarrassing secrets we would rather not have exposed. We challenge people to live for God and to follow His standards as revealed in Scripture. But none of us is perfect. Perhaps it would be better if those of us in the limelight could be more honest about our shortcomings and our battles with temptation. But I don't think Christians are willing to accept that, even though all of us, new Christians and old, struggle to be all that God wants us to be.

A further complication for some Transition Christians is their profession. An entertainer, a movie star, a professional athlete, or a popular author who accepts Christ is often expected to change professions by some Christians. He's supposed to give up his livelihood and travel the Christian circuit giving his testimony. But businessmen or teachers or doctors aren't expected to change professions just because they've had an encounter with Christ. If Christians would only think it through they would realize that their logic is faulty.

For those better-known "celebrities" who come to Christ, I plead with the Christian community to have patience. Don't push them into the limelight. Give them time to grow spiritually. I know that for the length of time I've been a Christian, my spiritual growth is probably not what it should be. I was rushed too quickly into the ministry. I should have been discipled and trained far more than I was.

I believe the local church should protect such a vulnerable Christian. Some older, mature believers should take such a person under their wings and give him time to grow. Before a celebrity Christian is allowed to give his testimony, the church should make sure he gets some training. No one ever showed me how to give a testimony. Somehow I was supposed to learn it by osmosis. It would have saved me much embarrassment if someone had sat down with me and showed me, step-by-step, how to present my testimony and how to give an invitation. And it would have meant a great deal if that person had also helped me learn how to grow spiritually while I was on the road, ministering to others.

It's very common that the Transition Christian has a desire to minister to his former associates. It was logical for me to want to reach out to atheists. I understand atheists and how they think. Likewise, I return occasionally to meetings of Alcoholics Anonymous. I think the Christian who comes out of alcohol abuse or drug abuse or homosexuality or whatever problem does a major disservice if he doesn't return to that support group, whether it's AA or PDAP or SOS or whatever the organization. It's important to go back and be a witness of what Christ has done in his life. Newcomers need to see and hear someone who's been sober for many years say, "Twenty years ago I crawled in here as a drunk. Now I own my own business and I'm an usher in the church and I give 5000 dollars a year to the church because that's what I used to consume each year in alcohol."

That kind of statement is a powerful witness. He doesn't have to say, "You're going to hell unless you accept Christ." Just being there, saying he attends church, and showing how he's now a productive member of society is a tremendous witness.

Some Transition Christians want to do even more than that. Practically every time I speak, someone comes up to me and says "I'm a reformed alcoholic" or "I'm an ex-homosexual" or ex-whatever, and he's thinking about starting a ministry in that area. My answer is always, "If you feel God calling you, then do it. But be sure you can support yourself financially, because as a Transition Christian you won't find it easy to raise support."

It's frustrating, but there aren't a tremendous number of church people jumping to support such ministries. So I encourage Transition Christians to find another source of income to supplement the giving. For me, a major source of income is the sale of books by mail order. Besides my own book, *My Life Without God*, I have sold tens of thousands of books by various conservative and evangelical authors. I tell Transition Christians I don't want to discourage them, but I feel they need to be prepared because the road won't be easy. But I would never recommend that a person not go into the ministry if he really feels that God is calling him. If someone is a reformed drug-user and he decides to have a ministry to drug-users and only one person is saved as a result, it was worth the effort.

Another reason why it's important for a person to return to minister in his former area of problem is the language. The subcultures of substance-abusers, homosexuals, and promiscuous people have their own vocabulary by which they identify each other. They also understand the uniqueness of that lifestyle in a way that an outsider can never fully comprehend. It's almost impossible for an ex-drug addict to help an alcoholic for the simple reason that an alcoholic spends hours getting high whereas the substance-abuser often gets high within 15 to 20 seconds of a hit. What the alcoholic does is often socially acceptable, at least until he does something obnoxious. It's perfectly all right to sit around in the bar; he can legally buy his drug. The drug-abuser cannot legally purchase his drug. He cannot consume his drug in public. Often the cost of his addiction forces him into crime to support his habit. Likewise a former homosexual cannot minister to a prostitute. She will never feel he understands. So I encourage Transition Christians, if they feel led by God, to go back to their subculture to minister to those they understand best.

Unfortunately, the church may recognize the need for a specialized ministry but not realize that the resource for meeting that need is often right there within the congregation. For instance, a church may conclude that there is a drug problem in the community and that they need to start an antidrug program. They decide to hire someone to manage the program and to reach out to drug addicts and former addicts in the community. Having made that decision, they contact the nearest seminary and have a job announcement put on the bulletin board. Since there are always seminarians nearing graduation who are looking for jobs, the church will have plenty of applicants.

The problem is that there are rarely any former drug addicts in seminary. The people potentially best qualified for the job are probably right there in the pews. They have already graduated from the school of hard knocks. They know more about drug addiction and rehabilitation than any seminarian will ever know. All they need is some encouragement, some support, definitely some training, and perhaps even time to attend seminary on a part-time basis while they start the ministry.

If this sounds so obvious, why don't more churches hire such people? There are probably many reasons. One is that these people won't run a "traditional" program that the church finds comfortable. Who knows what kind of new people they will bring into the congregation? Some of the things they do could be potentially embarrassing. Rather than risk that unknown, most churches would rather hire a traditional minister. Often, as a result, the most effective ministries to these specialized groups are not in churches but through specialized parachurch organizations.

One church that recognizes the power of using their own people for ministry is Bear Valley Baptist in Denver, Colorado. Under the leadership of Pastor Frank Tillapaugh, they have identified many "target groups" within the inner city of Denver. These are groupings of people with common lifestyles that are different from the mainstream of middle-class, conservative, evangelical churches.

Once a target group is identified, the church doesn't rush out to hire someone to minister in that area. "We . . . wait for the Holy Spirit to lead someone into that ministry," Pastor Tillapaugh writes in his book *Unleashing the Church*. He calls this approach a "relaxed concern." The need is usually met by someone from the congregation who feels God's call to that area of need. "When someone shares that he feels called of the Holy Spirit to begin a ministry to a certain group, pastors and the church as a whole should listen carefully."[1] In addition to more traditional programs, this church has specialized ministries to such groups as street people, international students, musicians and artists, and singles.

Unfortunately, I find that many churches are more comfortable when such "oddballs" settle into the mainstream of the church and society. When a Transition Christian says he feels a call to reach out to his former friends who are drug-users or homosexuals or alcoholics, the pastor will usually give him some encouraging words, but the unspoken attitude is that "this is just a phase; it will pass." Because the call isn't taken seriously, no help is forthcoming from the church.

I would urge that the church listen when one of its members feels God calling him to a specialized ministry. If someone says he feels a call to minister to homosexuals, and the church doesn't have a ministry directed to that need, then it should help that person find out if this is truly a call from God. This can be done by finding out what churches or organizations are already ministering to homosexuals in the city. Arrangements should be made for the member to spend time with one of those ministries, to find out how it operates, and to get some firsthand experience. If the call is real, he may choose to participate in one of those existing ministries. If he feels he needs to begin his own separate ministry, he has learned from experience what is being done, the logistical problems, what needs are unmet, and what is already well covered.

Transition Christians are a tremendous source for ministry. If the church is serious about reaching people in their communities who are not churched, it needs to encourage this great resource. Don't let them flounder and make the same mistakes others have made. Come alongside and provide what resources you have. Encourage them. Disciple them. Support them financially and with volunteer help. And pray that God will use them in a mighty way. Be assured that God will do just that!

1. Frank R. Tillapaugh, *Unleashing the Church* (Regal Books, 1978), pp. 51-52.

10

CHRISTIANS IN ACTION

A private Christian school in Pennsylvania had invited me to speak on the issue of "prayer in school" at a fund-raising dinner. The principal of the school asked me to include some quotes from the Founding Fathers so that their intentions regarding this constitutional issue would be revealed. Because of my family's involvement in the removal of prayer from the public schools in 1963, I felt qualified to give such a message.

I began my talk by discussing the framework from which the Founding Fathers drafted our Constitution. I discussed the background of our forefathers and the Christian education they received. I tried to show how they had modeled the new Constitution after the electoral system of Moses: "You shall select out of all the people able men who fear God, men of truth, those who hate dishonest gain; and you shall place these over them, as leaders of thousands, of hundreds, of fifties and of tens" (Exodus 18:21).

Within minutes I realized that my audience had no idea what I was talking about. They knew what Moses had done, but they did not understand the electoral system of the United States. I stopped my lecture and asked the group of some 500 people, "How many of you have a copy of the U.S. Constitution in your home which you could check to see if what I am saying is correct?"

A total of 22 people, less than 5 percent of the audience, raised their hands. Astonished, I asked those who thought *perhaps* they had one somewhere to raise their hands. No one did. I then asked how many people had ever heard of the Federalist Papers. Less than ten people raised their hands.

Certainly this had to be a fluke, I determined. So for the next four or five meetings as I spoke around the country, I asked my audiences to indicate by a show of hands how many

149

of them had a copy of the U.S. Constitution in their home. In every case, less than 5 percent raised their hands.

This is a national tragedy. Such ignorance of the people concerning the institutions of government ultimately allows those institutions to dominate them. With fear for our republic, I decided to do something about it. I began printing copies of the U.S. Constitution and distributing them to individuals, groups, and bookstores throughout the country. In a period of five years, more than 1.4 million copies were distributed.

It's amazing to me how many Christians ignore the U.S. Constitution. They view it as only a political document. It is not solely a political document and it was never meant to be. Our forefathers literally gave us a mandate from God on how to govern our country, and they used the Bible to design our system. (*The Making of America* by Skousen is a well-researched book which documents this process.)

Some people are uncomfortable with my conservative politics. They seem to think that such activism is incompatible with my work as an evangelist. They imply that Christians should not be involved in politics. To this I respond, "Then who *should* be involved? The atheists? Is that who we want running our government?"

As far as my conservative beliefs, I became an economic conservative *before* I was a Christian. Certainly my leftist, Marxist family background didn't lead me that way, but I discovered that my mother's convictions didn't match my experience. My mother was never able to hold a job; for her the American system didn't work. It made sense to her to try to change, even destroy, the system. Ironically, she used the very political process she despises to try to destroy that system.

From my mother I learned to appreciate the political process. But my experience in the business world gave me a different perspective. I found that society worked for me. When I worked hard and cooperated with my employers and those in authority, I made a good living. Life was good for me, so why shouldn't I appreciate the system that provided me with a decent life? So I did further study of some of the liberals my mother admired, and I found that they were usually mis-fits. Karl Marx was never able to hold down a job, and he wrote *Das Kapital* in a total alcoholic haze. Adolf Hitler's national socialism was directed by hatred toward a Jewish prostitute who had given him venereal disease. Whether it was Marx or Hitler, far-out principles were linked to people who were unable to function inside the mainstream of society.

Thus I became a political conservative. I appreciated our system of government and even ran for Congress in Austin, Texas, on the Republican ticket and managed to receive 46 percent of the vote. So when I became a Christian, I was aware of the importance of politics to the economic well-being of a nation.

My faith added another dimension to this awareness—the spiritual, which influences our moral values. I found among some Christians a misconception that to be Republican is the same as being Christian. That is a dangerous assumption. I was certainly not a Christian when I became a Republican. There are Christians among both the Republicans and Democrats, and there are non-Christians in both parties. Republicans are economic conservatives, not necessarily moral conservatives. However, the two can mix naturally and did so for a while, with great success. That's also why the Republican Party collapsed during the 1986 elections.

A major reason why Ronald Reagan was elected in 1980 and the Republican party gained a majority in the Senate was because of a major coalition between economic conservatives and moral conservatives. Coalitions have historically been the great strength of the Democratic Party. The Democrats have been able to take diverse groups and bring them together politically. For example, the pro-abortion group doesn't natu-rally fit well with blue-collar America, which is basically anti-abortion. But by promising the abortion people their right to abortions, and by promising blue-collar workers their right to union power, they merge these two diverse groups into a powerful political unit.

In 1980 Admiral Jeremiah Denton of Alabama tracked me down at a hotel room in Honolulu and pleaded with me to make a radio commercial for his Senate campaign. The purpose of the commercial was to show that he was going to work to return prayer to public schools. He convinced me of his sincerity to get God back into our schools and return America to a moral path. He was elected.

In 1986, Senator Jeremiah Denton had the President of the United States on his side as he ran for reelection. Not only did he not request the help of moral conservatives, but individuals such as Jerry Falwell and I were specifically told that we were not welcome. He didn't want me or any other fundamental Christian organization coming near his campaign. And surprise—he lost the election. He lost because he broke the coalition that had put him in office.

In fact, every Republican senator who lost in 1986 lost for that same reason. The Republicans felt that the success of their economic platform had finally, at long last, given them popular support. Actually, the economic conservative element of the Republican Party represents only about 40 percent of the population. It needs the *moral* conservatives as well if it hopes to become the majority party.

Both economic conservatives and moral conservatives need each other. The two groups don't seem to understand that they share a common problem. When economic freedom disappears as socialism encroaches, spiritual freedom also disappears. And if you take away spiritual freedom, you also take away economic freedom. You must have *both* economic and spiritual freedom in order to have a truly free society. We have two groups working for the same goal, yet for the most part they are separate from each other. As a result we make little progress.

However, something that concerns me even more than a coalition between conservative groups is our understanding of and involvement in the political process. There are some areas of vital concern to Christians, and we have the resources to address those areas through the political process. But because so many Christians do not understand how our system of government works, they are frequently ineffective.

I believe it is a Christian's responsibility to understand the government of his nation, whether he lives in the Soviet Union, Saudi Arabia, the United States, or any other country. In the United States, an astonishing number of citizens do not understand our form of government. Children learn in school that the United States is a democracy. *That is not true.* The United States is *not* a democracy; it is a republic.

In a true democracy, whatever a majority of the people decide is the law. If 51 percent decide that blacks can't vote, then blacks can't vote. If a majority decide that it's illegal to be Baptist, then all Baptist churches are closed down. Whatever is the will of the people at a given fleeting moment is what is done in a democracy.

Fortunately, our republican form of government is based on a Constitution that is inviolable. This document states that certain rights belong to all citizens and cannot be changed. This is what protects the rights of minorities in our nation. Our Constitution is what makes the United States a republic, and this is what makes us a great nation. Americans must understand this or risk losing their freedoms.

A further problem is that many Christians do not understand how to work effectively within the process of government. Often they do a great deal in areas that are relatively meaningless. For instance, for many years Christians thought that sending petitions to the President was the answer. So they worked hard in presidential years to elect a man like Ronald Reagan who would back their political agenda. The problem is that the President of the United States has little power domestically. Sure, he prepares a budget for Congress and he has considerable influence. But he cannot determine domestic policy. For example, President Reagan is strongly opposed to abortion and favors returning voluntary prayer to public schools. But he has actually been able to do very little to change the laws concerning these two areas.

The House and Senate, of course, have much influence, but even there they don't control many of the things that happen in America. For example, the policies for zoning of our churches are handled by individual cities, towns, and counties. Our public schools are controlled by 3700 school districts in the United States. The issue of what is taught in schools is handled by school boards and state legislatures. None of these things are handled by the President of the United States. Yet Christians go out in droves to elect a godly man as president, but when it comes time for the city council election, some back-room, cigar-smoking, beer-drinking clique can get an entire city council and mayor elected because most Christians don't bother to vote.

I spoke to a church in upstate New Jersey where the pastor told me how he and his congregation had spent nine years battling severe zoning restrictions. The church had been unable to add a building, expand its parking lot, or even put up a new sign. The town was 25 miles from a military base which provided a lot of business for the community, primarily through several bars and nightclubs. The political machine that controlled the city council was primarily interested in keeping those servicemen happy. They viewed any church expansion as a threat to that source of revenue.

"How many people do you have in your church?" I asked the pastor.

"We have about 900 people; we're the largest church in town," he answered.

"And what's the population of this town?"

"About 7000."

"So over 10 percent of the population are members of this church. Let me ask you another question: How many people voted in the last city council election?"

The pastor didn't know, but one of his elders answered, "There were about 1100 votes cast."

Instantly I saw the solution to his problem. It was obvious! "So what you're telling me is that *anytime* you want to control the city council, you can. If you want only Christians from your church on the city council, all you have to do is run five people. If every single member of your church votes, you can have every city council slot, every school board slot, the mayor—you'd never have to worry again about this being a godly town."

The pastor's jaw nearly hit the table. For nine years he had battled this political machine, totally unaware that his church had the means to change the problem anytime it wanted to do so.

This is also true on a large-scale level. In Dallas, the city council passed a series of zoning restrictions that made it impossible for churches to build in residential areas. They would have to build new buildings in commercial areas, literally on strips between factories. Though pastor after pastor testified against the new zone code, it passed. This is incredibly ironic, since probably two out of three residents of Dallas are Baptists. If the churches didn't want this kind of treatment from the city council, all they had to do was elect an entire Christian city council.

Christians need to realize that change comes from the bottom up. Our country is not run by some nebulous machine back in Washington. It's run by the city councils and county commissioners and school boards and state legislatures.

Some people are learning to recognize the difference. For many years the church fought pornography in Washington D.C. with petitions to the President and to Congress. Meanwhile, the problem of pornography escalated. What finally began to put a dent in the problem was when people realized that they could do something on the grass-roots level. Jerry Falwell led a boycott of Seven-Eleven Stores which forced them to remove pornography from their shelves. It's on the grass-roots level that the church can be most effective.

Antiabortion groups have also discovered that they can do a lot on the local level by working directly against specific abortion clinics. In Texas they've demonstrated that the people running abortion clinics are profiteers. They aren't providing a social service; abortion is a major and profitable industry. And whereas hospitals must meet all kinds of regulations in order to be in business, any slipshod physician could open an abortion clinic. So abortion foes lobbied the state legislature and a law was passed that makes it more difficult for such operators to open this type of business.

Another area is prayer in school. It depresses me when I think of how much money has been spent in Washington D.C. to return prayer to the public schools. If that money had been used to pressure school boards to provide equal time for legally permissible Bible reading and prayer activities in the schools, we would have many schools with better behavior habits.

The fact is that laws are in place right now to do what I just mentioned. The Equal Access Law requires that any school that has an extracurricular activity program *must* provide the same facilities to religious groups that it provides for non-religious groups. In other words, if the school allows Future Farmers of America, student council, and Young Republicans to meet within the school building, then it must also allow a Christian club or Hebrew club or other student-led religious group to use the facilities.

This law has met with so much hostility that many schools ignore it entirely. One school system in Massachusetts did away with its entire extracurricular program rather than allow religious meetings inside their school buildings. But most schools will not take such a radical stand. If Christian students want to start a voluntary, student-led program, the law allows them to do so. A strong Bible study and prayer group on campus provides a base for witnessing by the students within that school. And this means a lot more than a few seconds of required prayer each morning, a ritual which most students find meaningless anyway.

If Christians want to change things in their community, they can do it. The minimum we should do is *vote* in local city council and school board elections. But we should also attend city council meetings, PTA meetings, and school board meetings, and then voice our views there. This is where changes are made on the local level. If such bodies consistently refuse to respond to our complaints, then let's exercise the right we have to elect representatives who do reflect our perspective.

In Houston the city council passed an ordinance giving medical benefits to the live-in lovers of homosexual city employees. This so infuriated Christians that enough signatures were collected on a petition to force the issue onto the ballot. In the election, the law was repealed. This issue could not have been resolved in Washington D.C.

We've talked about our responsibility as Christians to our country. But I also feel we have a responsibility to the world. I believe that our form of government is the best in the world, and I believe we should be willing to spread the news of our system around the world. The Communists believe in their system enough to promote their way of government. And they've been very convincing. It troubles me that we go to such great efforts to take the message of Jesus Christ overseas in order to help people find spiritual freedom, but we don't help people become physically and mentally free as well. Sure, we must spread the gospel. But when we share the gospel with a person who's spiritually, mentally, and physically shackled, do we only tell him that we've come to give him spiritual freedom? "That's fine for you," he says. "You're free; I'm still shackled."

We tend to think that all anyone needs is to be free spiritually. But we in America don't really believe that. I know of no Christian in the United States who is willing to give up all of his other freedoms in order to have only spiritual freedom. We are mentally free, we are physically free, and we are spiritually free in this country because we are protected by our Constitution.

The Communist missionaries are so successful because they understand this fact. They claim they will free people physically. Actually, they are taking the shackles off people, adding several links of chain, and then reshackling them. In the process they take away even the possibility of spiritual freedom. I would like to see Christian missionaries more aware of this area, able to minister to the total person.

Perhaps because I have seen and heard of the atrocities of Communists I feel a deep commitment to do something as a Christian. A poster hangs in my office to remind me of the true character of the enemy. It's a picture of a nine- or ten-year-old Afghan child without any hands. Across the top of the poster is the word "DISARMAMENT." Below the picture it says "Soviet Style." Americans don't realize the vicious tactics of the enemy. The Soviet Union has dropped exploding toys onto villages in rebel-controlled areas of Afghanistan. When children pick up these toys and play with them, they explode in their hands. The idea is that by wounding the children, the men are taken out of combat because they're forced to stop fighting and take care of their children. The use of these devices is well-documented. It's been condemned by the Red Cross and every other major international body except the United Nations.

Americans need to understand the viciousness of the enemy. They need to understand that the Soviet Union is a satanic state controlled by satanic ideas. We need to realize what is happening in places like Afghanistan because if we don't, someday it will happen here. And we need to help where we can. I have worked with the International Medical Corps, which has vast experience inside Afghanistan. My organization has collected medical supplies for use in their facilities and clinics inside the country and on the border in Pakistan.

My greatest area of foreign involvement has been in Nicaragua. I have long had a sympathy for the fighters who are trying to regain freedom for their country of Nicaragua. This Central American country has suffered under the cruel Communistic dictatorship of Daniel Ortega. I had heard numerous horror stories of the suffering of these people. A pregnant woman and her two children tried to cross the river into Honduras and were machine-gunned down by Communist troops in Nicaragua. When the soldiers came down to inspect their prey, they discovered that the woman was pregnant, cut her open with a bayonet, took the unborn child, stabbed it with the bayonet, and waved it in the air for all to see. They then stabbed the two children and left.

Miraculously one of the children, a little girl, survived despite bullet and bayonet wounds. Some Honduran soldiers, having watched this whole episode, crossed the river and brought this child to safety. She was flown to Texas for medical help and she continues to live there today.

For a while I was content to realize that our country was giving aid to the struggling Contra resistance effort. Then in August of 1984, confused by propaganda from the Nicaraguan government and certin liberals, Congress ended all aid for Freedom Fighters in Central America. For the last few decades, when a country has fallen to Communism the United States has encouraged the people of that country to revolt. But we have done little to help these people in their fight. And when they did revolt and establish a provisional government—in Hungary and Czechoslovakia, for example—we did not support them. We stood back and watched them get trampled by Soviet tanks.

It's incredible to me that we have done so little to resist the spread of Communism, yet every Communist revolution has received overwhelming support from the Soviet Union. I got involved because if our government would not support the Contras who wanted freedom from their oppressive government, then the American people would have to do the job. If only we had gone to Nicaragua 50 or 75 years ago with a missionary zeal to spread the ideas of our form of government! We could have shared the gospel of Jesus Christ and seen them have mental, physical, *and* spiritual freedom.

In an attempt to help, I set up an organization called Freedom's Friends and gathered some medical supplies for the Contras. I was invited to come to Honduras to observe distribution of those supplies. While there, I was introduced to Enrique Bermudez, General of the rebel army, at the command headquarters of the Nicaraguan Democratic Force (FDN). I had brought a couple of cases of Spanish New Testaments with me, and on Saturday afternoon I asked him if there was a chaplain or priest to conduct church services on Sunday, and if I might distribute the New Testaments then. He said there were no chaplains and no services and gave me permission to lead a service at 10:00 A.M. the next day.

The next morning as I got into the chow line, I noticed a group of men sitting on several large tree stumps in the area where we would hold the service. I couldn't imagine what the men were doing there instead of eating breakfast, so I went over to talk with them. "Why are you men gathering here so early in the morning?" I asked one soldier.

"Some gringo preacher is going to tell us the word of God," he answered. "We want to make sure we are close enough to hear." It was three hours before the service was scheduled to begin! In the United States I've never heard of anyone showing up three hours early for a church service.

By 10 o'clock hundreds of people were present, including soldiers, officers, family members, and friends from the surrounding area and other camps. They had no idea who I was, but they were hungry for spiritual food. I was not confident of my Spanish, so I recruited a Cuban-American to translate my message. Then I presented the basic gospel story of how Jesus Christ had come to pay the penalty for our sins, and how we can enjoy salvation through Him.

At the close, I asked those present who wanted to do so to repeat a salvation prayer with me, inviting Jesus Christ into their hearts. Then I asked those who had prayed to raise their hands, and hundreds of hands went up. After the service I gave away all my Spanish New Testaments. I could see tears in the eyes of Enrique Bermudez as he said to me, "Do you have a copy of that prayer? I would like that for myself, for I said those words."

A few hours later I went to the Commandant's tent, and as I walked past the guards I saw him lying on his cot with the prayer rewritten in Spanish in one hand and his Bible in the other. That experience convinced me that it was my Christian responsibility to help free these people in one way or another. In further talks with General Bermudez and many other Contra leaders, I learned just how intolerable life had become under the Sandinista regime. It's hard for us to imagine what it's like without freedom. We can go to our nearest airport, buy a ticket, and fly to almost anywhere in the world. No one is going to stop us from leaving this country. As a result, there are probably 5000 people who want to come into the United States for every one who leaves.

How bad do you think things would have to get in the United States before you said, "I cannot stand this anymore" and you packed whatever you could carry and left the country? In Nicaragua, 15 percent of the population of three million people have fled the land of their birth since 1979! How many more would leave if they could? Some 400,000 Nicaraguan refugees are massed near the borders of Nicaragua in Honduras and Costa Rica.

Ironically, the church was promised freedom in Nicaragua prior to the Communist takeover. But that was a lie. If you are a preacher in Nicaragua, your sermon must be approved by the Bureau of Religion and Cults. You must write your sermon and submit it ten days in advance of delivery. If it is approved, two armed soldiers sit in the back of the church and listen to you give it on Sunday morning. If you vary from the pre-printed sermon that was approved by the board of censors, those two soldiers arrest you and take you away. Most likely, you'll never be seen again.

The amount of religious persecution, and persecution of people in general, is unbelievable. If there is an unauthorized church meeting either in the church or in a home, soldiers may invade and gun down the participants. Or they may set fire to the building and machine-gun the people as they try to escape. In the Contra camps I heard story after story about persecution simply because someone went to a church that didn't preach the government line, or because someone was related to someone who had fallen into political disfavor. Many testimonies of torture were too gruesome to repeat here.

Besides providing medical supplies and preaching the gospel, in 1984 Freedom's Friends began a Christmas gift campaign. We asked people to gift-wrap a box for a child. Items such as a toothbrush, toothpaste, a comb, shoes, and articles of clothing, as well as small toys, hard candy, and crayons were received from all over the United States. In 1986 we received and distributed more than 20,000 presents from all 50 states, Canada, Japan, and several other countries. For most of these children, these were the first Christmas gifts they had received in more than five years.

The Transition Christian should be, and many times is, involved in fighting the expansion of godless Communism. There are tens of thousands of Transition Christians who have turned from Communism. At nearly every church where I preach, I am approached by at least one person who was saved out of Communism. These people know that Communism doesn't work.

I am not advocating that every Christian must get involved in the Nicaraguan problem or help Afghan refugees. I am not saying that every Christian needs to run for political office. But I am asking, "What is our responsibility as Christians?" I believe that we all have a responsibility to understand our form of government, to be acquainted with the contents of our Constitution, and to vote in local, state, and national elections. Further, if we are not pleased with the work of our elected officials on any level, or if we do not approve of certain government policies, let's get involved and do something about it. We can work to elect people who will represent our point of view.

Finally, we must not just think selfishly about our own comfort within our own country. We must recognize our responsibility as "ambassadors of Jesus Christ" to help others around the world. And what should we do as ambassadors? The words of Christ Himself are a fitting way to conclude this discussion. In a parable where He described the final judgment, where He will separate the sheep from the goats, He stated our responsibility:

> Then the King will say to those on His right, "Come, you who are blessed of My Father, inherit the kingdom prepared for you from the foundation of the world. For I was hungry, and you gave Me something to eat; I was thirsty, and you gave Me drink; I was a stranger, and you invited Me in;

naked, and you clothed Me; I was sick, and you visited Me; I was in prison, and you came to Me." Then the righteous will answer Him, saying, "Lord, when did we see You hungry, and feed You, or thirsty, and give You drink? And when did we see You a stranger, and invite You in, or naked, and clothe You? And when did we see You sick, or in prison, and come to You?" And the King will answer and say to them, "Truly I say to you, to the extent that you did it to one of these brothers of Mine, even the least of them, you did it to Me" (Matthew 25:34-40).

11

THE CHURCH IS NOT FOR PERFECT PEOPLE

I've been told that I tend to be rather blunt in my assessments, and that is probably evident in this book. However, my purpose in writing this book is not to condemn but rather to encourage those who, like me, have come to Christ later in life, and to help the church understand us better. Transition Christians are not a new phenomenon. In fact, the first-century church began with them. While some early converts grew up in the Jewish faith, those who were Gentiles certainly didn't. They came out of pagan cultures that often were even more hedonistic than ours. Indeed, at the beginning of the church, our Lord said, "It is not those who are healthy who need a physician, but those who are sick; I did not come to call the righteous, but sinners" (Mark 2:17).

Over the last 20 centuries there have always been adult converts. Some of them were rather famous, like Saul and Augustine in the early church, and more recently people like C. S. Lewis and Chuck Colson. But the assimilation of such new believers has never been as easy as it was in the first century, for after the first generation of Christians there arose another kind of Christian, one who grew up in the church. He met Christ at an early age, learned all the rituals, memorized Scriptures, and learned how to pray and do all the "right" things.

Ideally, when a Transition Christian enters the church, someone takes him by the hand and teaches him the essentials of the faith and the traditions of that body. For every Paul that enters the church under "suspicious" circumstances, there is a Barnabas who comes along to encourage him and introduce him to the members.

Unfortunately, that didn't happen in my case, and it frequently doesn't happen to other Transition Christians I know. If nothing else, I hope this book introduces the two sides and brings us into a deeper fellowship.

In light of what I've written, I'd like to state some principles I think have emerged from my experience and those of other Transition Christians. Most of these principles relate directly to the Transition Christian, but they will also help the church understand their needs. A few are recommendations to the church at large to consider some adjustments that will make its ministry more relevant.

1. *If you have prayed a salvation prayer, and you have publicly stated that you intend to live for Christ, yet you are not sure you are saved, assume you are and act accordingly.*

It was nearly a year before I finally settled on the fact that I was a new person. Jesus Christ had died for me—for Bill Murray. He really had come into my life.

People who accept Christ as adults often have recurring doubts about their salvation experience. Every time they stumble and repeat some sin from their past, they wonder how Christ could possibly accept them in their wretched condition. They don't recognize those thoughts as from our enemy, Satan himself. Satan would try to convince us that we only had an emotional experience and that none of this is real.

Further, our minds and bodies have been programmed by the world for so many years. With a few dramatic exceptions, those patterns aren't obliterated just because Christ has now come in. Satan would have us believe that nothing has changed. But it has! Jesus Christ has now entered the picture, and for the rest of our lives He will be in the process of changing us.

If you have prayed, acknowledging to God that you are a sinner and that Jesus Christ died for you, and you have invited Christ to come into your life, then accept as *fact* that He has done just that. If you need more assurance, then go forward at a church service that gives an altar call and make your commitment public. Make it public by being baptized. Make it public by telling some people in the church about your decision. In this way you identify with the church. When the doubts assail you, you can point to those times when you stood for Christ publicly.

Finally, move on from that point. Read the Bible. Pray. Learn what it means to live for Christ and show your love for Him by your obedience to His commands. Assume that your commitment to Him is a *fact* and move ahead. Recognize that life hasn't changed except in one crucial way: You will continue to face many, if not all, the temptations that assailed you before you were a Christian; the only difference is that now you don't have to give in to those temptations. Now you have power available, in the form of the Holy Spirit, to keep you from sinning. When you fail, it's not because God wasn't with you, but because you didn't look to Him to give you victory over the temptation.

2. *Don't be blinded by human failures in the church.*

This is a common trick of Satan. He not only tries to convince us that we're not saved, but he loves to argue that no one else is saved either. "Look at all the hypocrites in the church," is a familiar line. *And it's true.* The church is full of hypocrites, and inevitably the Transition Christian spots them. The one who's had a drinking problem will quickly meet someone in the church who is still drinking. The young man who has struggled with promiscuity will meet some young church lady who tries to seduce him. Satan would love to convince us that this is proof that the church is not real.

The bumper sticker which some Christians have on their cars is most appropriate: "Christians aren't perfect, just forgiven." The church is made up of people. All of us have struggles with the world. Not one of us is perfect, and we won't be perfect until the day we meet Christ face-to-face. So let's admit that fact and try to understand and help each other as we let Christ teach us how to have victory over the world.

3. *Make Christ the center of your life, not the church.*

When the church is the center of our lives, it's easy for human beings to disappoint us. Christianity is about *Christ*. It's about developing our relationship with *Christ*, and the church exists to help us understand and further that relationship. If we make church activities the center of our faith, we miss out on the joy of a relationship with Christ Himself.

A relationship with Christ doesn't depend on how many church dinners we attend, or our participation in the church bowling league. Events like that are Christians enjoying life together on earth, not the salvation experience. The center of our life must be Christ, and the church should make every new convert aware of that quickly. If a pastor sees a new Christian getting involved in too many church activities, he should help that person realize he's substituting church for Christ.

4. *Accept responsibility for your own spiritual growth.*

This builds on the previous principle. It's tempting to expect other people to meet our spiritual needs, and when that doesn't happen, to blame the institution—usually the church—for the problem. It's also tempting to think that if you're single, finding a mate will make you complete. Only Jesus Christ makes us complete. And we can experience that completeness only when we accept responsibility for our own growth.

So if the church is not meeting your needs, go to the pastor and talk about it. Or find an older, wiser believer who will counsel you. If you need a support group because of a divorce or a substance-abuse problem, take responsibility for finding that support group. It may mean going to another church. Often a pastor, when he knows your needs, will encourage such a move because he wants to see you grow too.

No one can make us grow. No one is going to make us read the Bible or pray. No one will make us join a Bible study. But we need these things; we need to make them a part of our routine. If you can't do it, ask for help. There are mature Christians who would be glad to help. You may not find someone the first time, so keep asking.

I am very thankful for Pat Cummins, pastor of the Furgusson Road Baptist Church, who for several years patiently counseled me whenever I had questions. Because of my travels, I would often call him late on Sunday night after speaking at a church. I would tell him about some question or issue a person had raised that I couldn't answer. With my Bible open, Pat would guide me to the answers in the Word.

5. *As much as possible, control the environment of your children.*

It's not unusual for the Transition Christian to experience tremendous tension in the home. If there is a non-Christian spouse in the home or with visitation rights, the children usually take sides. Therefore it is important, if at all possible, to discuss the issue of your children's moral and religious training with that spouse in order to (hopefully) come to some kind of agreement.

If the Christian parent has authority over the children, he should use it to maximize their exposure to the Person of Jesus Christ. If the children are going to accept and love God, they must first see the love of Christ in their parent. And they must be exposed to other Christians their age. This means taking the children to church and Sunday school whether they want to go or not. It may also mean switching them from a secular school, where there are a lot of drugs and alcohol and other negative influences, to a school that has a better environment.

We can't make a child believe what we have come to believe, but we can remove him or her from the negative elements and expose him to the Christian. If you were involved in drinking, your kids probably hung around with the kids of your drinking buddies. Now that you're going to church, you need to get your kids away from the old influence. This will cause conflict, but the Transition Christian can't back down.

The issue is control. If you're in charge of the home, then you make the rules. If I go to a hotel, that hotel has rules. I can't run around the halls naked. They want me to wear bathing trunks in their pool. If I don't want to follow those rules, then they ask me to leave. Likewise, you need to inform your kids of the rules. If necessary, post them on your refrigerator. If a child protests, talk it out with him, but with the understanding that ultimately you have the last word.

6. *Remember that you are saved, but never forget what you have been saved from.*

It's so easy to forget where we've come from as Christians. Especially after a few years in the church, we forget how bad our life of sin really was. That's dangerous because it makes us more susceptible to sin again. It also makes us less tolerant of those who are struggling with the same problems we once had, when what they need is for us to understand their struggles and minister to them.

For someone who's had a serious problem, a support group is very important. All support groups for substance-abusers, child-beaters, spouse-beaters, rapists, and others have this in common: Over and over they are reminded of how bad it really was. For the parent who hasn't hit her child for five years, she forgets how bad that practice was until a brand-new parent enters the group with tears streaming down her face and tells how she hit her child and broke his nose and she had to take him to the hospital and lie about how he was hurt. Then the reformed parent remembers, "That's what I did too!" It keeps her from slipping back into the same attitudes that once caused her to hit her own child.

7. *Sin takes time, and it takes time to rid yourself of sin.*

It takes several hours to get drunk. It takes time to steal, sell to a fence, find a pusher, buy drugs, and then take those drugs to get high. It takes time to find a willing person when you want a new sexual partner each night. Sin takes time.

When a sinner comes to Christ, he needs to quickly find things to replace the time he used to spend in all that sin. He can't be expected to just sit at home in his rocking chair and watch television if he used to hit the single bars every night. Many reformed alcoholics and drug-users get involved in intricate hobbies their first year. Even better is to get involved in a cause. There are many ministries that need volunteers. People with time on their hands can man phones, pack boxes, stuff envelopes, type letters, or maintain facilities. They can replace their old activities by helping to further the work of Christ.

8. *All ministers need a practical education about substance abuse and other problems in our society.*

By ministers, I don't just mean ordained pastors. *Anyone*

who wants to reach out and minister to those in need must know what sin is. Of course, this doesn't mean that they need to have committed every sin. But they need to understand the horror and the pain of being trapped by addiction or lust or greed. They need to see people going through heroin withdrawal. They need to hear the stories from kids whose dads beat them when they were drunk, which was almost all the time. They need to hear the alcoholic tell about how he schemed to get more money to buy another bottle of booze. They need to hear a prisoner tell how he got caught up in a life of crime. That's the disease. These are the people we are called to minister to. It isn't pretty.

Most ministers have no idea what these problems are like because they grew up in a healthy family with a loving mother and father. Yet most kids today will live at least part of their childhood with a single parent. Millions of kids suffer scars from sexual molestation or physical abuse. Husbands and wives are being battered by their spouses. Old people are being beaten by their adult children. These things are happening not just in ghettos, but in our suburbs, in upper-middle-class communities. We need to learn about these problems so we have compassion as we help people gain victory over the power of sin.

I believe that every seminary needs to bring in people from prison, from the child-abuse support group, from Alcoholics Anonymous, and from drug-abuse treatment programs to speak to its students. It needs to send seminarians out to the field to talk to prostitutes and rapists and drug-users. I'm sure many of these young men and women would be shocked by what they see and hear. But these are the people they will someday have to minister to.

9. *Don't judge people by their material success or lack of it.*

People tell me, "Boy, are you lucky; you get to fly all over the country." To them my life looks glamorous. The fact is that I go crazy cooped up inside an airplane. I fly an average of 20,000 miles a month. I often pace up and down the aisle, or else listen to gospel music on my tape recorder while I work on my computer. Each night I sleep in a different hotel bed. Sometimes I wake up in the middle of the night and I'm not sure what town I'm in.

I say this to make the point that while my life may look glamorous on the outside, much of it is drudgery. People don't see the preparation and hard work and even tears that go on behind the scenes. I find that this is true for almost every successful person: There's a price that was paid for the cheers or the fame or the wealth. People see that a couple lives in a mansion, but they probably don't realize that the man of the house has to work 80 hours a week in order to have that nice home. They don't see the tension between husband and wife or with their kids. They don't realize that underneath the success there is a desperate emptiness.

We don't need more things; we need Christ. "I know how to get along with humble means, and I also know how to live in prosperity," wrote the apostle Paul (Philippians 4:12). Paul could write this because Christ was the center of his life. Jesus Christ is the One who gives life meaning, and we can have Christ whether we're wealthy or poor.

10. *If you're called by God into the ministry, go!*

I believe I was called by God to be an evangelist and to minister to atheists. I believe He also placed me in Nicaragua to see the suffering there, and He directed me to take those Christmas presents to the Nicaraguan children. This doesn't mean that I necessarily like doing those things all the time. But I really have no choice; if God calls, I must obey Him.

All Christians are called to have a ministry of some form. A few of us are called to make the ministry a full-time profession. It isn't easy, and there are always people who will try to stop us. I have dents from mortar rounds in my bulletproof vest to prove it! There are all kinds of stumbling blocks to the ministry. Satan doesn't want us working for God, and he won't let us do it without a fight. We need to be prepared for that fight.

I opened this book by demonstrating the contrast between the old Bill Murray and the new. God has done a great work in my life since January 24, 1980. But He's not through with me yet! He still has a lot of work to do.

I'm glad the church is not for perfect people. If it was, I wouldn't qualify. Fortunately, the Perfect One, Jesus Christ, is Head of the church, and He is in the process of changing all of us. If we remember that, then surely we can be more patient with each other.

For the new adult Christian with all the excess baggage from his past, let's thank God for the work He's started in this person's life. And let's allow God to use us to help build this person to maturity. But we must be *willing to be used*, and we must be willing to admit that we too are in the process of maturing in Christ.

I can't change the facts of my past. I've done a lot of things that I'm not proud of. Some of it was because of my background, but most of it was because of my own sinful nature. Yet Christ died for me, and He's forgiven everything I've ever done wrong. Still, I'm continually reminded of my past. I can't think of my daughter Robin without realizing the consequences of my sin. But on the other hand, I can't look at my daughter Jade without thanking God for how much He has already changed me. With that encouragement I'm willing to trust Him to finish the job in me. I'm also willing to believe that someday, just as God did a miracle in me, He can also do a miracle in the lives of people like Robin and my Uncle Irv. And yes, even my mother!

ABOUT THE AUTHOR

William J. Murray is the founder and director of Freedom's Friends, an organization which supplies the medical and spiritual needs of refugees from Communist countries. He is also the president of the William J. Murray Evangelistic Association in Coppell, Texas.

Besides his bestseller *My Life Without God*, Murray has written *Nicaragua: Portrait of a Tragedy* and has edited a special bicentennial edition of *The Complete Constitution of the United States of America*.